MW00364634

DOMINIC BRADBURY • PHOTOGRAPHY BY RICHARD POWERS

THE ICONIC AMERICAN HOUSE

ARCHITECTURAL MASTERWORKS SINCE 1900

728.37
Brad

WILLIAMS LIBRARY
1515 N. SERVICE
CLAREMONT 7017

DISCARD

Contents

Introduction
8

Introduction

The concept of the 'American Dream' encompasses the broad ideal of a better way of life. It offers a fresh start, an honest job and, above all, a home to call one's own. In America, the idea of building a home for oneself and one's family has always had an extraordinary resonance, beginning with early settlers on the East Coast, followed by adventurers pushing West. For many, the dream would never be complete without a house and a roof over one's head.

The pioneer spirit has been a vital spur towards construction and creativity, from prairie cabins to brownstones, and everything in between. The American vernacular was, in itself, a creative fusion drawn from the experience of the English, Dutch, Spanish, and many other incomers, fabricating an architectural approach that was both a new invention and a reworking of European ideas, styles and influences. It was old and new at the same time, with its form

and character also shaped by context. Farmhouses and barns, for instance, would be built with local materials such as timber or stone, and woven into the landscape with logic and practicality in a way that would help protect the building and its occupants from the elements.

In the modern era, the combination of this pioneering spirit and an openness to ideas and incomers has helped to forge some of the most important and influential houses in the world. There was a constant willingness to experiment and innovate, which helped to secure America's prominent position on the architectural map and send its fresh ideas back into the wider world.

Early in the 20th century, the novelist and designer Edith Wharton, along with her architect Ogden Codman, Jr, argued for an American version of pared-down neoclassicism. Wharton's home in Massachusetts, The Mount (1902; p. 14), was infused with French

Frank Lloyd Wright, Fallingwater (1939), Mill Run, Pennsylvania.

9

Above, left to right Edith Wharton and Ogden Codman, Jr, The Mount (1902); Greene & Greene, Gamble House (1909); Richard Neutra, Kaufmann Desert House (1947).

Opposite, left to right Ludwig Mies van der Rohe, Farnsworth House (1951); Ricardo Legorreta, Greenberg House (1991); Philip Johnson, Glass House (1949).

and Italian influences, yet the fluidity of its rooms and openness to the landscape were, arguably, distinctly American. In California, Greene & Greene (p. 20) also offered a unique version of Arts and Crafts, creating homes that were open to their surroundings, naturally ventilated and incorporated the latest technology, such as electric lighting.

By the 1920s, American architecture and design was making its mark. In Chicago, Louis Sullivan, who coined the phrase 'form ever follows function', created a new generation of steel-framed skyscrapers. His former employee, Frank Lloyd Wright, went on to design a series of variants of the American home, including the 'Prairie' and 'Usonian' houses. Wright's take on an 'organic architecture' was most fully expressed at Fallingwater (1939; p. 54). By then he was famous around the world, with disciples who would pay to watch him at work and learn from the master.

Like so many others, architects from Europe, Scandinavia and other parts of the world were drawn by the promise of the American Dream. American architecture benefited from the arrival of many talented émigrés, including Rudolph Schindler (p. 26), Richard Neutra (p. 72), Albert Frey (p. 226) and Eliel Saarinen (p. 36), all of whom added, in their own way to the richness of American design and encouraged greater innovation.

Some, like Saarinen, were not only architects, but also educators. Walter Gropius (p. 48), Marcel Breuer (p. 192) and Ludwig Mies van der Rohe (p. 108) were the most famous of the Bauhaus exiles, having left Germany shortly before the Second World War, after the Nazis had shut down their cradle of early Modernist thinking. All three transferred to the US, bringing with them a design philosophy forged in Europe, but adapted to the context of America.

Gropius and Breuer took inspiration from the New England landscape, while Mies developed his vision of modernity in Chicago, with buildings like the Lake Shore Drive Apartments. Mies was the greatest exponent of what his acolyte Philip Johnson described as the 'International Style', a crisp, linear way of building for the modern age. With Farnsworth House (1951), in Plano, Illinois, he created one of the greatest exemplars of postwar Modernism: a floating pavilion of glass and steel.

Mies's work encouraged the evolution of many other important buildings, including Johnson's Glass House (1949; p. 102) in New Canaan, Connecticut, and the steel-and-glass pavilions of Craig Ellwood (p. 222) in California. Ellwood, Charles and Ray Eames (p. 96), and others played a key role in spreading the message of Modernism through participation in the famous Case Study Programme, which featured exemplary new houses that were published and promoted in the pages of *Arts & Architecture* magazine.

Yet, as evidenced by the wild richness of American mid-century Modernism, the field of architecture and design in the United States was a broad church. It welcomed crisp proponents of the Californian Modern style, the Subtropical Modernists of Florida and the southern states, and the followers of a more expressive, organic approach, such as Bruce Goff (p. 78) and Bart Prince (p. 248). All were welcome, and all added to the rich variety of the American home.

During the postwar world of the 1950s and '60s, the power and vitality of American architecture and design was almost unrivalled. The country's infrastructure and manufacturing capacity escaped the Second World War almost unscathed, allowing a rapid transition to peacetime production. Mid-century American design was full

of ideas, imagination, colour, pattern and warmth, enriched by a vibrant process of multi-disciplinary cross-pollination. Designers such as Russel Wright (p. 150), Eero Saarinen (p. 120) and others designed not only houses, but also the furniture to put inside them, creating a cohesive version of American style, with communities like Palm Springs, California, and Columbus, Indiana, becoming micro-centres of design.

During the 1960s and '70s, even as corporate America thrived, there was still an experimental edge to architecture and design. Robert Venturi (p. 168) and Denise Scott Brown, the authors of *Leaving Las Vegas*, became the godparents of Postmodernism, with a 'less is a bore' approach to cherry-picking from art history. The work of Charles Gwathmey (p. 204) and Peter Eisenman (p. 236) suggested that there was still breadth, as well as depth, to American residential design.

The pioneer spirit of architectural adventurism was, and is, still alive and well in America. The work of Rick Joy (p. 296), Steven Holl (p. 290), Thomas Gluck (p. 278) and others offers an imaginative response to landscapes of great diversity, beauty and vulnerability. Their residential designs are almost as varied as the landscape itself, yet share not only a respect for context and the land, but also playful and thoughtful references to the vernacular.

The houses in this book chart a journey across America and across time, embracing many different aesthetics and expressions of form. Yet they are all iconic houses, meaning that they have an influence and resonance that goes well beyond the original brief and artistic conception. They are shining landmarks within an American architectural dreamland – one that is full of life, drama and invention.

Above, left to right Peter Eisenman, House VI (1975); Kendrick Bangs Kellogg, High Desert House (1993); Steven Holl, Ex of In House (2016).

Opposite Charles Gwathmey, Gwathmey House & Studio (1965).

The Mount

LENOX, MASSACHUSETTS

Edith Wharton & Ogden Codman, Jr (1902)

Above The formal gardens were designed by Wharton to complement the grounds of the house, which is entered via the rear courtyard.

Opposite The stone steps leading to the terraces sit within the sense of symmetry and order set out by Wharton and Codman.

The collaboration between Edith Wharton and architect Ogden Codman, Jr began in the 1890s, when the writer asked Codman to design the interiors of her home, Land's End, in Newport, Rhode Island. It was the beginning of an important friendship, and an alliance based on a mutual love of French neoclassicism and a suspicion of the excesses of much 19th-century residential design.

Wharton and Codman also collaborated on what was the first published book for each of them: *The Decoration of Houses* (1897). Becoming both successful and highly influential, it took a holistic view of architecture, interiors and landscape design, while promoting the 'laws of harmony and proportion'.

'The supreme excellence is simplicity,' Wharton and Codman concluded. 'Moderation, fitness, relevance – these are the qualities that give permanence to the work of the great architects ... There is a sense in which works of art may be said to endure by virtue of that which is left out of them, and it is this "tact of omission" that characterizes the master-hand.'[1]

A few years later, at the very beginning of the 20th century, they began working together once again, applying their philosophy of design to an ambitious new house and the surrounding gardens. Wharton and her husband Teddy had acquired over 100 acres of land near the town of Lenox, and she and Codman began designing a house that took inspiration from French and Italian neoclassicism, yet also embraced a number of innovative characteristics.

Tucked into the sloping landscape, the house is accessed at the rear, where the entry sequence leads into the lower level of the building, giving the entrance a semi-subterranean character, and then up to the principal level, which unfolds in dramatic fashion. A long, vaulted gallery runs along the back of the house, overlooking the courtyard, with terrazzo and marble floors leading to the formal living spaces. These are arranged within an enfilade that connects, via a sequence of French windows, to the adjoining terraces, which overlook the gardens, designed by Wharton, and a lime walk forming a pathway between them.

Opposite The elegant gallery forms a key axial line linking the living spaces on the main level of the house; the floors are in terrazzo and marble.

Below Upon entering, visitors are greeted by a fountain featuring the god Pan, before ascending the stairs to the principal storey above.

The central drawing room is neoclassical at heart, with its French marble fireplace and ceiling mouldings. Yet this generously proportioned space is lifted by the quality of light, a level of restraint that comes from the 'tact of omission' and a relative purity of line. Like the dining room and library to either side, the drawing room flows out towards a long terrace, which came into its own during the summer months as a natural extension of the living spaces, where Wharton liked to play ping pong with her guests.

The library features floor-to-ceiling bookshelves, with the books providing the main 'decoration'. Wharton usually preferred to work in her bedroom upstairs (*The House of Mirth* and *Ethan Frome* were both written

here) and organize the running of the house from there or the adjacent private sitting room. Traces of wallpaper found during restoration suggest that this may have been one of the few parts of the house where Wharton and Codman allowed extraneous pattern and departed from their usual dictum that architectural detailing should be simply expressed and stand upon its own merits.

As a whole, The Mount can be seen as kind of laboratory where Wharton and Codman gave life to their ideas. The interior spaces have a fluid quality, while the number and size of the windows means that the house feels light and fresh, offering constant glimpses and views of the gardens. Wharton herself claimed that she was a better landscape

Below The oak-panelled library was mainly used for entertaining visitors; much of Wharton's writing took place upstairs in her bedroom.

Right The drawing room is one of the most generous spaces in the house, with three sets of French doors leading out to the adjoining terrace.

gardener than a writer, while her friend Henry James (who often visited The Mount) described it as 'a delicate French château, mirrored in a Massachusetts pond'.

Following a breakdown in Teddy's health and the deterioration of their marriage, Wharton began to travel increasingly to Europe and eventually moved to France, where she lived from 1911 onwards. The house and gardens have been sensitively restored and are now open to the public.

[1] Edith Wharton and Ogden Codman, Jr, *The Decoration of Houses* (1897; New York: Rizzoli/Mount Press, 2007).

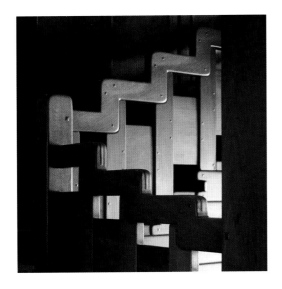  

Gamble House

PASADENA, CALIFORNIA
Greene & Greene (1909)

Above Artisanal craftsmanship shines through in every detail of the house, from the staircase to the stained glass and electric lanterns.

Opposite The exterior fuses elements of Swiss mountain chalets and Japanese architecture with an elegant Arts and Crafts aesthetic.

In the early 20th century, Pasadena, situated at the northern edge of greater Los Angeles, was known for its fresh air, green spaces and views of the San Gabriel mountains. One of its neighbourhoods was 'Little Switzerland', an area close to the Arroyo Seco ('dry canyon'), itself home to Brookside Park and the Rose Bowl Stadium.

Little Switzerland took its name not just from the topography, but also from the wooden chalet-style homes that dominated the neighbourhood. The most famous of these is the Gamble House, one of the finest exemplars of the Arts and Crafts style in America. There is something of a Swiss influence to the building, yet it also takes some conscious inspiration from Japanese architecture and garden design.

The architects, brothers Charles and Henry Greene, became key figures within the American Arts and Crafts movement, which was founded in part on the design philosophy championed by William Morris and John Ruskin in England during the late 19th century. In the US, the West Coast designer and publisher Gustav Stickley promoted the Arts and Crafts aesthetic, with its use of natural, handcrafted materials over factory-made products, through his furniture and in the pages of *The Craftsman*, a journal founded by Stickley. The Greenes were contributors, and shared many of its values.

'Let us begin all over again,' wrote Charles Greene in 1907. 'We have got to have bricks and stone and wood and plaster: common, homely, cheap materials, every one of them. Leave them as they are ... why disguise them? The noblest work of art is to make these common things beautiful.'[2]

Having founded their architectural practice in Pasadena in 1894, the brothers designed a number of houses in the area over the following years. The firm was the natural choice for David and Mary Gamble, when they decided to build a new winter residence for themselves in Little Switzerland. David Gamble was the wealthy son of the founder of Procter & Gamble, based in Cincinnati. He and Mary had three children to take into consideration, as well Mary's sister ('Aunt Julia'), who spent a good deal of time with the family.

Below The staircase and window seat are largely in mahogany and teak, with Sarouk rugs adding colour and pattern.

Opposite In the living room, most of the furniture was made by Peter Hall Manufacturing Co., with additional pieces by Stickley.

The design of the house, arranged over two main levels, seeks vibrant connections to the gardens and surroundings. There are front and rear terraces at ground level, as well as three sleeping porches alongside the bedrooms on the upper level. These shaded, fresh-air retreats with a view provide a halfway point between inside and out.

Importantly, the architecture and interiors were treated by the Greenes as two sides of the same coin, within one cohesive *Gesamtkunstwerk* – a total work of art. The house is a hymn to the beauty of wood of all kinds, the characterful tones and grains of which lend the building much of its character. The woodwork is both highly crafted and intelligently detailed, with rounded edges that soften the interiors throughout.

The ground floor is dominated by generous living spaces with large fireplaces, overlooking the gardens. Iridescent glass windows and door panels with Japanese-style vines and creepers adorn the dining room and hallways. Smaller spaces like the study and a guest bedroom are at the front.

While its Arts and Crafts aesthetic looks to the traditions of the past, the Gamble House is also a modern home. In many respects, it sits at the junction between old and new. Most striking of all is the sense of synergy with nature, seen in the use of natural materials and the layered connections between the Japanese-influenced garden and the house, which is open to the public.

[2] Linda G. Arntzenius, *The Gamble House* (Los Angeles: University of Southern California School of Architecture, 2000).

Opposite The stained glass in the dining room is by artist Emil Lange.

Below 'Aunt Julia's' bedroom, seen from the sleeping porch alongside it. Julia Huggins lived with the family until the early 1940s.

Schindler House

WEST HOLLYWOOD, CALIFORNIA

Rudolph Schindler (1922)

Above The house features 'tilt-slab' walls, banks of glass and a series of 'sleeping baskets' on the roof, designed by Schindler.

Opposite The gardens were seen as an integral part of the communal life of the house, with outdoor rooms, complete with fireplaces.

With the design of this house in West Hollywood, Rudolph Schindler proposed nothing less than a new way of living. Influenced by the benign Californian climate, camping trips to Yosemite and visits to the pueblos of New Mexico, he suggested a 'co-operative' model for the home he shared with his wife Pauline, her friend Marian Chace and Marian's husband Clyde. The result has often been described as the first truly modern house in America.

Born in Vienna, Schindler studied under Otto Wagner and Adolf Loos at the Academy of Fine Arts, where he also met Richard Neutra (p. 72). At an early stage, he became aware of the work of Frank Lloyd Wright (p. 54) and emigrated to the US with the aim of finding a job in the master's Chicago office. It took some time, but eventually Wright did bring him into the fold and Schindler became an important part of the practice, especially while Wright was in Tokyo, working on the Imperial Hotel.

In 1920 Wright asked Schindler to move to Los Angeles to supervise the construction of Hollyhock House for Aline Barnsdall,

a philanthropist and patron of the arts. Schindler and his new wife settled in California, but within a few years he decided to form his own practice in Los Angeles. Schindler House was one of his first and most influential solo projects.

Clyde Chace, a skilled builder and engineer, had experience of tilt-slab construction – a new way of building in which concrete was poured into flat, timber moulds on site, and then the 'cured' slab walls were levered into place. With modest loans from the bank and Pauline's parents to fund the project, Schindler chose to use the tilt-slab system for the new, single-storey house.

He developed a pinwheel plan with three spokes, two of which – one for each couple – held studio spaces, with banks of glass between the concrete slabs framing views of the landscape. The third arm held a guest bedroom and a garage; a communal kitchen sat close to the axis of the pinwheel. There was no conventional sitting or dining room, and bathrooms were small and minimal. Throughout, the avoidance of any kind of ornamentation created an austere aesthetic.

'The basic idea was to give each person his or her own room,' Schindler explained, 'and to do most of the cooking right on the table, making it more of a social "campfire" affair than a disagreeable burden for one member of the family.'[3]

Much of the interaction between the four residents took place outside, with the pinwheel formation helping to partially shelter and enclose two patio gardens. Schindler created outdoor rooms here, complete with fireplaces. These fresh-air spaces were complemented by summer 'sleeping baskets' up on the roof, where spider-leg timber frames supported canvas awnings. Here, the idea of camping out was re-created by Schindler and combined with an elevated position among the treetops and overlooking the gardens.

As an experiment in informal co-operative living, Schindler House was not a great success. Clyde and Marian Chace moved to Florida in 1924, just a few years after it was completed, to be replaced briefly by Richard Neutra and his family. Pauline, too, moved out for a time, before returning in 1930 to live in a separate portion of the pinwheel.

Schindler himself continued living and working in the house until his death in 1953. The house remains a key exemplar of early American Modernism, pioneering not just a new tectonic approach, but also an original approach to what Schindler called 'space architecture' and a more intimate relationship between inside and out.

[3] Kathryn Smith, *Schindler House* (New York: Harry N. Abrams, 2001).

Opposite The studios are simply designed, but lifted through a vibrant relationship with the garden, which provides light, air and vivid greenery.

Below A sense of aesthetic austerity characterizes the interiors, but texture does thrive in the choice of materials, including concrete and timber.

Wharton Esherick House & Studio

MALVERN, PENNSYLVANIA
Wharton Esherick (1926)

Above This autobiographical home and studio can be seen as a narrative that has evolved over time within its rural woodland setting.

Opposite The entrance 'tower' and spaces alongside it, including the elevated terrace, were the most recent additions to the building.

Like his career, Wharton Esherick's house and studio evolved and changed over time. The building's final phase was completed in 1966, yet this highly individual home, gallery and workshop was first conceived by the architect back in 1926, inspired by the natural, organic character of the local barns. By the mid-1960s, the house and studio had become his masterpiece, encapsulating many of his ideas about art, sculpture, furniture and interiors within one idiosyncratic and dream-like home.

Drawing upon a modest inheritance, Esherick had bought a small farmhouse nearby in 1913 with his wife, Letty. The house stood within five acres of farmland and woods, from which Esherick tried to make a living, although funds to support the family were often tight, sometimes leading to the farmhouse itself being rented out to paying guests.

In 1926 Esherick built a stone-walled studio, pushed into a gentle hillside and surrounded by trees. Like his early pieces of sculpture and furniture, the original studio has an Arts and Crafts influence, offering a crafted echo of the past. The 'barn' originally held

Esherick's wood-working studio, as well as space for storing timber and larger pieces of work. Over time, he added a small bedroom above the studio, 'sculpting' the space and its integrated furniture from locally found timber. A few years later, he added a log garage nearby.

'I always say that if I can't make something beautiful out of what I find in my backyard, I had better not make anything,' said Esherick, who gradually moved away from an Arts and Crafts style to a purer, more expressionistic and sculptural aesthetic approach. 'I was impatient with the contemporary furniture being made – straight lines, sharp edges and right angles – and I conceived free angles and free forms, making the edges of my tables flow, so that they would be attractive to feel or caress. So I suppose it is called "free-form" furniture.'[4]

Gradually, as Esherick began to secure a small but dedicated clientele, as well as interiors commissions, the studio began to grow into a home. He added a bedroom for his son, Peter, for use when Letty and their daughters were working in repertory

Below The house has a highly organic quality; nearly all of the furniture was designed and made by Esherick, including the 'rail sofa' from 1959.

Right The building is a diary of the architect's work: the flat-top desk was made in 1929 (the top replaced in 1962), and the drop-leaf desk dates from 1927.

theatre and the farmhouse was let, as well as a dining room, all contained within a wooden addition to the stone barn. In 1956, Esherick's architect friend Louis Kahn (p. 156) designed a small, separate workshop next door. Finally, in 1966, Esherick designed and built a tower alongside the wooden section of the house and studio, creating additional spaces that included a new kitchen, which flows out to a deck that floats above the hillside and looks out into the trees.

The house, therefore, serves as a kind of diary, or journal, with three or more chapters. Yet, within, it feels entirely cohesive and organic, unified by the use of many different varieties of timber and Esherick's 'free-form' approach. The characterful interiors

Below A twisting ladder stairway rises to the attic-style bedroom at the top of the house; the sinuous sofa was made for a client in 1936, but rejected.

Opposite The dining area, in one of the 'newest' parts of the house, leads out to an elevated terrace overlooking the woods. The oak table dates from 1967.

have a crafted warmth, comparable with the work of George Nakashima (p. 144) and the Scandinavian mid-century modernists, but also a kind of biomorphic quality, with elements such as the extraordinary staircase, itself reminiscent of a whale's spine and ribs. As such, the house feels as though it has grown from the hillside itself, yet there is also a clear ergonomic logic to the interiors and a great attention to detail, down to the carved coat pegs on the walls.

'I have said over and over again that just because you are spending your energy making something beautiful, it doesn't have to mean that it cannot be functional,' said

Esherick, who became known as the 'dean of American craftsmen'. 'When I am creating a chair, for example, I continue to try it out by sitting on it to see that it is comfortable. My design follows function.'[5]

The house is now owned and cared for by the Wharton Esherick Museum, which has opened it to the public. Inside, the curated collection of furniture also serves as an informative and engaging survey of the gradual evolution of the architect's design philosophy.

[4] Visitor information at the Wharton Esherick Museum.
[5] Ibid.

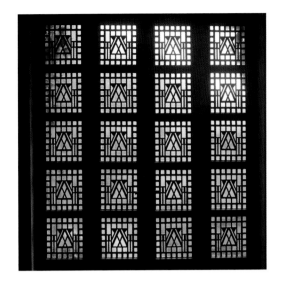

Saarinen House

BLOOMFIELD HILLS, MICHIGAN

Eliel Saarinen (1930)

Above The courtyard and terrace to the rear of the house offers a more secluded and private garden room, with sculpture by Wäinö Aaltonen.

Opposite Over the years, the house has softened into its campus setting, with Boston ivy adding a layer of greenery to the elegant brick façade.

The invention of the Saarinen House, cradled within the Cranbrook Academy of Art campus, was truly a family affair. It was home to its architect, the Finnish-born master Eliel Saarinen, and his wife, Loja, who designed many of the fabrics in the house and planned the surrounding gardens. Their daughter Pipsan was an interior designer, and developed a series of decorative paintings for the doorways of the upstairs landing, and their son, Eero (p. 120), was tasked with designing the furniture in the master bedroom, aged just nineteen.

But it was Eliel Saarinen who was at the heart of the house, while the building itself was at the centre of the Cranbrook educational community, a 315-acre campus in Bloomfield Hills, 32 km (20 miles) north of Detroit. Cranbrook was founded by George Booth, a newspaper baron, philanthropist and enlightened patron of Arts and Crafts architecture. It was Booth who entrusted Saarinen with the task of masterplanning and largely designing an assembly of buildings, which included boys' and girls' schools, a science institute, a museum and

a library, along with the Academy itself, which Saarinen headed until the late 1940s.

Saarinen House was completed in 1930, almost six years after the architect began working for Booth, whom he had met through Booth's son Henry, one of his architecture students at the University of Michigan. The house is often described as Saarinen's crowning achievement at Cranbrook, blending an Arts and Crafts exterior with an accomplished and layered Art Deco interior, seamlessly integrated into a unique and harmonious whole. It was a reminder that while Saarinen was masterful with the grander picture of community planning, he also had an exquisite eye for detail and was a true perfectionist.

Back in Finland, Saarinen had established himself as the country's leading architect, working in an Arts and Crafts manner. His reputation was spreading abroad when he entered the competition to design a new skyscraper for the Chicago Tribune. Saarinen came second, but his design was so widely praised that he was seduced into moving to America in 1923.

Opposite The dining room features a table and chairs designed by Saarinen; the rug and hanging lamp were also designed by the architect.

Below In the living room, the fireplace and torchères were designed by Saarinen, while the wall hanging, rug and upholstery are by Loja.

At Cranbrook, Saarinen soon established himself as an influential presence, not just as an architect, but also as an educator, overseeing the Academy and enticing and encouraging talents including Charles and Ray Eames (p. 96), Harry Bertoia and Florence Knoll, whom the Saarinens took under their wing to the point that she became part of their extended family. Alvar Aalto called Saarinen a 'bridge builder', and he was certainly one of those intriguing personalities who managed to span different eras of architecture, fusing Arts and Crafts, Art Deco and modernist influences.

Saarinen House also manages to combine aspects of traditionalism and modernity without a jolt. Designed at the same time as its neighbouring faculty house, the building has a discreet presence to the street, with the façade now covered in a vertical carpet of Boston ivy. Most of the windows on this side of the house, within a very public avenue of dormitories and other student and academic buildings, look into hallways and thoroughfares to preserve a sense of privacy. The larger windows and French doors to the back of the house, where it opens out to form a U-shaped plan around a large courtyard,

Opposite Within the seating alcove at one end of the studio, the textiles are all attributed to Loja Saarinen, while the hanging lamp is by her husband.

Below A seating alcove on the landing is graced with colourful designs by Saarinen; the luxurious master bathroom has an Art Deco flavour.

are partially protected by a covered porch to one aspect, and a studio wing to the other.

Inside, the couple created a series of rich, warm spaces with a wealth of colour, texture and natural light. Loja Saarinen, who ran her own weaving business in Bloomfield Hills and headed the Academy's textiles department, designed curtains, rugs and wall hangings, while her husband involved himself in every aspect of the interiors, from the finely detailed panelling and furniture in the dining room to the 'raisin and silver' tiled fireplace in the living room. He made good use of Cranbrook's own studios (opened in 1929, and later folded into the Academy) to commission pieces from resident craftsmen such as Swedish carpenter Tor Berglund.

But undoubtedly it was the studio that was the best-used and hardest-working part of the house: a large and flexible room, with space enough for a pair of draughting tables for husband and wife. These could be pushed back to the sides of the room for larger functions and parties, which the living room could not cope with. During a recent restoration process, furniture that had been scattered across the campus in the years after Eliel Saarinen's death in 1950, when the house was used by subsequent Academy presidents, was re-assembled and returned, along with paintings and artwork.

Morse House

LAKE FOREST, ILLINOIS

William Zimmerman (1932)

Above The metal frames of the windows, including the 'ship's prow' above the front door, are picked out in 'International Harvester Red'.

Opposite Over the years, the outline of the building has been softened by the maturing trees, yet its Art Deco character remains clearly visible.

In 1931, industrialist Robert Hosmer Morse became the head of Fairbanks, the family firm founded by his father, Charles. He had already held several posts at the company, as well as serving in the Signal Corps during the First World War, and went on to oversee the expansion of the business, while also becoming involved in other fields of engineering, from steam pumps to windmills.

Their main residence was in Chicago, but Morse and his family were tempted by the idea of building a weekend home in the town of Lake Forest, north of Chicago and not far from Lake Michigan. Lake Forest was, and is, an affluent area, punctuated with a number of forest preserves and golf clubs that lend it a semi-bucolic character. The family had set their hearts on Knollwood Circle, a combination of golf club and leafy residential estate, first laid out in the early 1920s by Samuel Insull, a business associate of Thomas Edison and a pioneer of early electrical utilities. Morse approached William Zimmerman, the former state architect for Illinois, to design an extraordinary new house here in the Art Deco style.

Assisted by his son and son-in-law, both partners at his Chicago-based practice, Zimmerman designed a sleek, modern home quite unlike any of the more traditional houses in Lake Forest. Often compared to a liner that has run aground in the woods, the substantial house has a crisp outline, interspersed with terraces and decks. The rhythmic window pattern within the irregular composition includes both horizontal bands and vertical punctuation, as well as pointed character windows above the front door and on the staircase, which resemble a ship's prow in miniature.

The house also features a covered rear porch on the ground floor, overlooking the garden, and a roof deck with a sheltered, shaded terrace up among the treetops. It is arranged across three principal levels, together with a substantial basement with a club or games room, plus a private bar with a speakeasy character. The central hallway leads through to the spacious living room, two steps down, with seating arranged around the focal point of the fireplace. Mirrored panels help to conceal heating

Below The sitting room retains its original fireplace and lighting. The furniture, sourced by the current owners, dates from the 1920s and '30s.

Right This alcove lounge, with sofas from the 1940s and the original passenger lift, sits to one side of the living space and overlooks the garden.

vents, while also enhancing the sense of light and space. A more intimately scaled annexe alongside hosts a secondary lounge, overlooking the garden, and a lift tucked away in one corner.

To the other side of the central hallway and staircase are the dining room, kitchen and service spaces. The main family bedrooms and bathrooms are on the floor above, with the uppermost level accommodating additional guest bedrooms and bathrooms, offering a total of eleven bedrooms and

Below In the sitting room, the original mirrored panelling has integrated heating vents, and the chair is a French Art Deco piece.

Opposite The master bedroom sits at mid-level, overlooking the gardens; the original bay has a series of windows that can be opened individually.

thirteen bathrooms. Integrated elements include a dumbwaiter, which runs between the kitchen and the basement clubroom, together with fitted benches at the bottom of the stairs with lift-up seats for storage.

The current owners instigated a sensitive restoration process both inside and out, which included stripping the layers of paint on the exterior walls and restoring the sandy-coloured stucco finish. Windows were also carefully restored and refreshed, using 'International Harvester Red' for the paintwork on the frames. Inside, restoration continued with layers of carpeting removed from the original Douglas fir floorboards on the ground floor. Previous owners had boxed up many of the Art Deco light

fittings, which were carefully unpacked and replaced, as far as possible, in their original positions. The choice of furniture and furnishings is also sympathetic, with much in the way of period French and European Art Deco designs.

The garden design for the five-acre parcel of land was undertaken by C.D. Wagstaff & Co., although only echoes of the original layout remain. A key point of difference between period photographs and the look of the house today lies in the way that the nearby trees have grown and matured, softening the angular outline of the building and giving it the feeling that it has settled gently into the landscape over the intervening years.

Gropius House

LINCOLN, MASSACHUSETTS

Walter Gropius (1938)

Above The linear form of the house stands out against the trees; to the rear, Gropius added a porch, which looks onto a Japanese-style garden.

Opposite The rectangular outline is joyfully eroded by the projecting entrance canopy; the external spiral staircase leads up to the roof terrace.

Walter Gropius, architect, educator and former director of the Bauhaus, arrived in America with his family in 1937. He had been tempted by an offer from Harvard University to modernize its architecture department, assisted by his friend and colleague Marcel Breuer (p. 192), who was also invited to become Gropius's partner in a new architectural practice. It was, in every sense, a new beginning.

The family home was an important part of this fresh start. It was situated on a four-acre site, between Cambridge and Boston, not far from Walden Pond, a gift from a generous patron and supporter, Helen Storrow. Gropius spent a good deal of time deciding on the exact position of the house, consulting with his wife and daughter about what features they would like to see included in the design. The result could be described as a fusion of early modernist thinking and a more contextual approach to the site, setting and region. Gropius himself was suspicious of the idea of an 'International Style', arguing in favour of buildings that were responsive, rather than simply didactic.

'When I built my first house in the USA,' he wrote, 'I made it a point to absorb into my own conception those features of the New England architectural tradition that I still found alive and adequate. The fusion of the regional spirit with a contemporary approach to design produced a house that I would never have built in Europe with its entirely different climatic, technical and psychological background.'[6]

The house adopted many characteristics associated with early modernist residential architecture, including a broadly linear outline, curtain walls, ribbon windows and fluid, open-plan living spaces. Yet Gropius was also determined to make the most of the bucolic setting, and adopted several regional influences. The house's timber frame was coated in clapboard, painted white, and there was a fly-screened rear porch, a brick fireplace in the living room and landscaping that made use of local stone.

The notion of a modern fusion was introduced by the entrance, which featured a distinctive projecting canopy, pushing out from the house at an angle, with a sequence

Below The entrance hall and stairway sit at the centre of the house, with the main living area to one side and kitchen and service spaces to the other.

Right The living space is largely open plan, with integrated bookshelves and furniture designed by Breuer. The study is visible through the open door.

of glass bricks to create a protective screen around the front door. The ground floor features a spacious living and dining area with a study to one side, separated by another wall of glass bricks. The compact service spaces and a maid's room are pushed to one end of the house, while a winding staircase leads to the upper level. Here, Gropius created two family bedrooms, a guest room and a substantial roof deck, with a secondary staircase leading back down to the garden. The semi-enclosed sun deck offers views out across the landscape.

Below The bedrooms are modestly scaled, with integrated shelving and wall lights; baton detailing is in keeping with the geometrical precision.

Opposite The upper storey has three bedrooms, two bathrooms and this dressing room, as well as the roof terrace, complete with sun deck.

Gropius incorporated modern furniture made from tubular steel and plywood, mostly designed by Breuer.

Visited by students and prospective clients, the house became a kind of laboratory, as well as a statement of intent. Breuer built his first American home nearby, and the two buildings helped shape a number of residential commissions the partners worked on together, before going their separate ways. Perhaps more importantly, this was a project tailored to the needs of Gropius's family, along with the setting. As a new beginning, it marked a thoughtful synthesis of avant-garde modernity with a more personal touch; Gropius's wife Ise said that the house fitted the family like a glove.

'No problem during the design process was ignored, or simply given over to a stale or inefficient solution,' wrote their daughter, Ati Gropius Johansen. 'No opportunity to appreciate beauty, whether natural or manmade, was ever missed. To many of my friends, when I was growing up, this house was indeed a curiosity. They loved to visit our unusual house, which was so different from theirs. I remember a woman who once asked my mother, "Mrs Gropius, don't you find it terribly exhausting to always live so far ahead of your time?"'[7]

[6] Walter Gropius, 'Scope of Total Architecture' (New York: Harper, 1955).
[7] Ati Gropius Johansen, 'Designed for Living', *Historic New England Magazine* (Fall 2003).

Fallingwater

MILL RUN, PENNSYLVANIA
Frank Lloyd Wright (1939)

Above The house offers a series of terraces and outdoor rooms that push out into the landscape; the ribbon canopy connects it with a guest lodge.

Opposite The horizontal bands of the building cantilever out over the stream; vertical lines of local stone anchor it to the site and provide spine walls.

Frank Lloyd Wright ran a fellowship programme at his two studios in Wisconsin and Arizona, which came to be known as Taliesen East and Taliesen West, respectively. One of the many apprentices that took part in the Taliesen Fellowship was Edgar Kaufmann, Jr, who later became director of the Industrial Design Department at the Museum of Modern Art, New York. Kaufmann introduced his father, a wealthy Pittsburgh department-store owner and patron of the arts, to Wright's work, and when the family decided to build a new weekend home in the Allegheny mountain range, Wright was the obvious choice.

By this time Wright was in his sixties, and his reputation had been well secured via a long and progressive sequence of residences, as well as by his writing, including an autobiography published in 1932. Wright had worked in various different contexts and settings, including Tokyo, where he spent many years working on the Imperial Hotel. But he was arguably most comfortable in rural settings, where his love of the natural landscape could be fully expressed.

The Kaufmann family owned a small cabin near a stream called Bear Run, a tributary of the Youghiogheny River, in western Pennsylvania, within a landscape of particular beauty. It was one of Edgar J. Kaufmann's favourite places, and it was here that he asked Wright to build a new house.

'There was a rock ledge bank beside the waterfall, and the natural thing seemed to be to cantilever the house from the bank over the fall,' Wright wrote later. '[Kaufmann] loved the site where the house was built and liked to listen to the waterfall. So that was a prime motive in the design. I think you can hear the waterfall when you look at the design. At least it's there and he lives intimately with the thing he loved.'[8]

With Kaufmann impatient to see designs for the house, Wright told his client that they were done and ready to be viewed, even though he had yet to put pen to paper. In just two hours, he famously sketched out what was already in his mind and presented the drawings to Kaufmann, who was delighted. Architect and client were also in accord with the principles of blending the house

In the living area, boulders push upwards through the flagstones next to the fireplace; fitted sofas reduce the amount of free-floating furniture.

into the site, with Kaufmann requesting additional features, including a plunge pool by the stream, which were integrated into the design. Yet nagging doubts about the structural athletics involved in building with reinforced concrete, a practice that was still in its infancy, would eventually cause tensions between Kaufmann and Wright. The addition of extra steelwork also compromised the structure, leading to problems that eventually required considerable repair works by the Western Pennsylvania Conservancy in 2002.

Reinforced concrete slabs were used to cantilever the house out over the waterfalls of Bear Run, while walls of local stone help anchor the building to the site. The concrete framework took the structural load of the façade, allowing Wright to create horizontal bands of glass that connect the house to the surrounding woodlands. The ground floor holds a large, open-plan living room and dining area, flagged with stone, which leads directly out to terraces to east and west, with the stream flowing underneath. The floor above holds three bedrooms and additional terracing, with the third storey devoted to

Below The bedrooms each feed out onto adjoining terraces, allowing the connection between inside and out to be maintained throughout.

Opposite The uppermost level holds a study and sleeping area; the 'Butterfly' chair (1938) is by Antonio Bonet, Juan Kurchan and Jorge Ferrari Hardoy.

a study and gallery at the top of the house. Wright also designed a guest house nearby, with a covered walkway connecting the master building and its satellite.

Fallingwater became the fullest expression of Wright's version of contextual, organic architecture, developed in response to the particular qualities and conditions of the site, setting and surroundings. 'It is the nature of any organic building to grow from its site, come out of the ground into the light – the ground itself held always as a component basic part of the building,' he said. 'And then we have primarily the new ideal of building as organic. A building dignified as a tree in the midst of nature.'[9]

The house also represented a clear alternative to the linear residences of the International Style, which Wright criticized for their sterility, and became a seminal building for architects of the postwar period, who embraced its organic approach to the full. For an increasingly environmentally conscious age, Fallingwater still has profound relevance, and is today one of the best-loved 20th-century buildings in America.

[8] Patrick J. Meehan, ed., *The Master Architect: Conversations with Frank Lloyd Wright* (Hoboken, New Jersey: Wiley-Interscience, 1984).
[9] Robert McCarter, ed., On and By Frank Lloyd Wright, *A Primer of Architectural Principles* (London: Phaidon, 2005).

Frelinghuysen Morris House & Studio

LENOX, MASSACHUSETTS

George Sanderson & John Butler Swann (1931/41)

The Frelinghuysen Morris House & Studio has often been described as New England's first truly modernist home. This unique rural retreat, created by artists George L.K. Morris and Suzy Frelinghuysen, drew inspiration from the work of the pioneering architects of the 1920s and '30s. With its crisp outline and linear form, it was a radical departure from the architecturally conservative Berkshires region and its great country estates.

Morris grew up at one of these estates, known as Brookhurst, where his parents had built a mansion in the Colonial Revival style. Their son, however, had very different ideas. Originally, Brookhurst totalled around 100 acres, but this has halved over time. The feeling is still bucolic, with an undulating landscape populated by firs, oaks, maples and silver birch, and room enough for Morris and Frelinghuysen to express themselves in their own unique way.

The studio was built first, in 1931, to a design by Morris's Yale classmate, architect George Sanderson. The modernist design was influenced by Morris's trips to Europe in the 1920s, when he studied with the Cubist artists Fernand Léger and Amédée Ozenfant, who worked in a studio in Paris designed by Le Corbusier.

Morris's time in the French capital helped to define his own distinctive style, and also shaped his love of modern architecture. The studio was designed and built on modernist principles, creating a double-height painting and exhibition space, partly toplit by skylights hosted by a sawtooth, twin-pitch roofline, supplemented by a substantial bank of glass to the front. The studio features a large fireplace and a mezzanine level to the rear, holding a small office.

Morris and Frelinghuysen married in 1935 and had an apartment in New York, where they were key figures among the 'Park Avenue Cubists'. A few years later, they decided to build a new house on the Brookhurst estate, alongside the studio. Morris asked a family friend, John Butler Swann, to design it, adopting a similar aesthetic approach to the earlier building. Swann built the house a little lower down the hillside, with a service area between the studio and house holding the kitchen, utility

Above Terraces alongside the sitting and dining rooms to the rear and glass blocks around the front door allow light to percolate through the house.

Opposite The original studio is on the left; the main house was added ten years later. A mural by Morris lines a walkway between the garages and the kitchen and service spaces.

Opposite The stairway features another mural by Morris; the sculpture on the plinth is also by him and is entitled *Configuration*.

Below In the sitting room, furniture designs by Alvar Aalto and Donald Deskey sit around the fireplace, flanked by two murals by Morris.

spaces and the side door; the garages are slotted into the hill, with a fresco by Morris decorating the covered walkway leading from the garage to the side door.

The main house also has its own dramatic front entrance, featuring a wall of glass bricks that allows sunlight to spill into the hallway, marble floors made of stone from the local Lee quarry, integrated ceiling light fixtures and fluorescent light tubes. The hallway leads straight through to a rear veranda, looking down into the woods. To one side there is a choice of taking a few steps down towards the main sitting room, or heading upstairs via a winding staircase,

graced with a mural by Morris. The ironwork banister here, also by Morris, was added later, after the couple noticed visitors hugging the wall on the way up.

The main sitting room is a generously scaled space in what is, in truth, a modestly sized house. The room features a picture window at one end, while another large window, with two side doors, leads out to a stone paved terrace. There are fitted bookshelves and cupboards, plus a small bar tucked under the stairs, and leather tiles on the floors. Furniture designs by Donald Deskey and Alvar Aalto sit around the fireplace, and there is room for a grand piano.

Below The use of glass brick in the master bathroom helps light to circulate, while also enhancing the modern character of the space.

Opposite Trompe-l'oeil frescoes by Frelinghuysen decorated her bedroom; here and elsewhere, drawers are integrated into the walls of the room.

The couple's art collection included works by Picasso, Braque and Miró, among others, although one of the Picassos (*The Poet*) was sold to Peggy Guggenheim to help fund the construction of the house.

The house itself became a canvas for art. The dining room features frescoes by Frelinghuysen, as does her bedroom suite. Her career as an artist was concentrated in the 1930s and resumed in the late 1950s, interrupted only by a second career as an opera singer during the postwar years. The rest of the murals in the house are by Morris, a founding member of the American Abstract Artists collective, and are more abstract in style. His career flourished during the 1950s and '60s, and he also became an art critic for the *Partisan Review*.

The spaces upstairs include a study, separate bedrooms for Frelinghuysen and Morris, together with a guest bedroom, all featuring much in the way of integrated bookcases and storage, which help to preserve the clean lines of the house. A link back to the studio from Morris's generous bedroom creates a thoughtful *promenade architecturale*, neatly tying the two structures together.

Alden B. Dow Home & Studio

MIDLAND, MICHIGAN

Alden B. Dow (1941)

Early on, it seemed as though Alden B. Dow was destined for a career with the family firm founded by his father. He studied mechanical engineering at the University of Michigan, and the expectation was that he would join the fast-growing Dow Chemical Company, based in Midland. But after three years, Dow decided to follow his heart and enrolled in the architecture programme at Columbia University. This was followed by a Taliesen Fellowship in Wisconsin, which confirmed his passion for organic architecture, together with its synergetic relationship between design and the natural world.

In 1933 Dow returned to Midland and opened his own architectural firm. One of his very first projects was his own atelier, situated on a parcel of land that formed part of the Dow family estate at the edge of town. The studio was carefully woven into the landscape with sensitivity and great imagination, using Dow's own patented 'Unit Blocks', made from concrete and painted white, combined with a wooden structural framework and an expressive, sculptural copper-coated roof.

The building's design was rooted in the landscape, working in harmony with the artificial pond created by Dow; the 'Submarine Room', in particular, which was used for meetings with clients, floats just above the water line. It also included a naturally ventilated, timber-framed draughting room, with echoes of the studio at Taliesen East, which Frank Lloyd Wright (p. 54) once described as an 'abstract forest'. Dow's own office alongside features a picture window that looks out across the pond and into the treescape beyond.

The studio expanded organically over several years, from 1934 to 1937, and was soon followed by the house, which was eventually completed in 1941. Arranged over two principal storeys, with multiple shifts in level and scale, the complex totals over 1,850 m² (20,000 sq ft) and offers a constant interplay between inside and out via sequences of windows, terraces and outdoor rooms.

Dow created a semi-distinct *promenade architecturale* for the house, which he shared with his wife, Vada, and their three children. The main entrance is set well apart

Above The house and studio are intimately woven into the landscape, with countless changes in level according to the shifting topography.

Opposite Dow used his 'Unit Blocks', made from cement and painted white, to form walls, sculptural chimneys and stepping stones across the pond.

Steps lead up from the main entrance of the house and into the spacious and open-plan living area, with its variety of seating zones.

from the doorway to the atelier, creating some separation between work and home. A processional set of steps leads up from the residential entrance into a generous, open-plan living space. Here, two seating areas lead upwards again, via three steps, to a lounge and dining area, as well as a screened porch to one side of the main living room, which cantilevers outwards dramatically over the pond below. A fully separate kitchen is also in this part of the house, with a guest suite beyond.

Along with individual bedrooms for the children and the master suite, positioned at the opposite end of the house to the guest room, there is also a choice of spaces for pleasure and leisure. These include a more private and intimately scaled secondary sitting room, a playroom (later re-purposed as an archive room) and a large games room. The playroom holds the main line of Dow's extensive model train set, while the locomotives of another branch can be glimpsed travelling around the ceiling space above the master suite. Like the studio, the house features countless integrated

Opposite The entrance to the studio leads into this reception area overlooking the pond; a few steps down is the 'Submarine Room'.

Below With its linear layout and banks of glass, the draughting room has echoes of Taliesen East; the lower level holds a lounge and home cinema.

elements, including fitted furniture and storage, which help lend a sense of order to the spaces and create cohesion, despite the complexity of the floorplan. The craftsmanship and detailing are also exquisitely executed, even though the materials themselves are seldom precious or pretentious. Loose furniture and lighting include carefully curated pieces by mid-century masters including Arne Jacobsen, Hans Wegner and George Nelson.

The design of the house, along with the gardens and grounds, also suggests the influence of Japan, which Dow visited in 1923, staying at Wright's Imperial Hotel. Dow returned after the Second World War,

and Japan remained a key reference point, in terms of both his architectural approach and his garden designs. The house and studio each have a strong organic sensibility throughout, as well as many playful and biomorphic touches. 'Nature relieves architecture,' he once observed. 'Architecture relieves nature.'[10]

Here at the Alden B. Dow Home & Studio, Dow created a micro-campus of a unique kind, layered with many complexities, yet it still manages to hold together as a single elegant entity, intimately connected to its surroundings.

[10] Diane Maddex, *Alden B. Dow: Midwestern Modern* (New York: W.W. Norton & Co., 2007).

Kaufmann Desert House

PALM SPRINGS, CALIFORNIA

Richard Neutra (1947)

Above Walls of stone tie the house back to the landscape, and a choice of terraces, bordered by breezeways, offer semi-sheltered outdoor rooms.

Opposite The main 'spoke' holds the master suite and main living spaces, which flow out to the pool terrace; the 'gloriette' can be glimpsed on the roof.

Edgar J. Kaufmann, department-store magnate and philanthropist, commissioned not just one, but two, of the most influential houses of the 20th century in America. After studying at Yale, Kaufmann took charge of the family's store in Pittsburgh and was a generous patron of the arts in the city. Encouraged by his son, an architect and later curator at the Museum of Modern Art in New York, he asked Frank Lloyd Wright to design Fallingwater (p. 54), completed in 1939. Just a few years later, he commissioned another extraordinary home, in the growing resort town of Palm Springs, California.

Edgar J. and Liliane Kaufmann's new home was intended as a winter retreat, primarily for the month of January, when the days are still warm and the nights are cool in the desert. This time, Kaufmann turned to Richard Neutra, whose career had taken off following the success of his Lovell Health House (1929), in Los Angeles. Neutra's work combined a modernist outlook with a contextual approach, along with a heartfelt belief in the power of architecture and design to promote wellbeing.

The couple secured a generous site next door to a house owned by the industrial designer Raymond Loewy, designed by Albert Frey (p. 226). Palm Springs itself was just beginning to take off at the time, a process that accelerated as it became a regular draw for the Hollywood elite, as well as fair-weather visitors from further afield.

Neutra's design was innovative in every way, and marked a significant evolution in his own work. The plan of the house created four spokes of a pinwheel, pivoting around a central circulation point. A semi-sheltered breezeway connected the carport to the entrance hallway, while another arm formed a guest wing. A third arm holds the kitchen, service spaces and staff accommodation, with the 'master spoke' hosting the main living spaces and the Kaufmanns' private suite.

The plan allowed the house to 'expand' to accommodate guests, who have their own private realm, or to concentrate upon the more intimate living experience offered by the combination of living spaces and master suite within one dedicated arm. Neutra expertly combined natural materials

Below The bedroom, with its compact en-suite bathroom, looks out onto the pool and garden via retractable walls of floor-to-ceiling glass.

Right The main living area, alongside the master suite, is an open-plan space with a dining zone at one end and seating at the other.

– such as timber and the sandstone for the chimney and retaining walls, which anchor the house to the land – and banks of glass. These transparent curtain walls offer a vivid sense of connection to the gardens, grounds and adjoining terraces; they include a glass wall in the living room – which retracts completely, allowing a seamless transition between inside and out – enhanced by the use of radiant heated floors that carry out to the pool terrace.

Above The dining area looks out onto a courtyard, which sits between the master pavilion and another 'spoke' holding guest quarters.

Opposite The 'gloriette' on the roof serves as an outdoor lounge and belvedere, with its own sun screen, seating and fireplace.

The Kaufmann Desert House offers, therefore, a new level of connection between inside and outside space. The sequence of outdoor rooms includes the 'gloriette' on the roof – a semi-shaded, open-sided space that forms an elevated belvedere, complete with a fireplace, for enjoying views of the landscape and mountains. This halfway space, somewhere between inside and out, adroitly managed to circumvent local planning restrictions, which limited the height of the building and ruled out a full second storey.

Neutra's design set a new paradigm for Desert Modernism. The linear form borrowed from the International Style, but the building also took inspiration from Japanese architecture and the compound pueblos of the southern states, while forging a fresh alliance between architecture and landscape. It became the ultimate mid-century escape – a dream home that encapsulates a rounded, glamorous vision of modernity. In the 1990s the house, which remains privately owned, was sympathetically restored by Los Angeles-based architectural firm Marmol Radziner, who respected and preserved its essential character, while updating services and amenities for 21st-century living.

Ford House

AURORA, ILLINOIS
Bruce Goff (1950)

Encapsulating Bruce Goff's enduring interest in organic design, geometry and 'found' materials, the Ford House is often described as his masterpiece. It is certainly a high point from his most imaginative and productive period during the 1940s and '50s, when he was also teaching at the University of Oklahoma, and stands out vividly among its more traditional neighbours.

From its completion in 1950, the house – also known as the 'Round', 'Umbrella' or 'Mushroom' House – has been a subject of fascination. It was commissioned by artist Ruth VanSickle Ford and her husband Albert (known as Sam), a civil engineer. Ruth Ford was also the owner of the Chicago Academy of Fine Arts, where Goff taught on occasion. The couple encouraged their architect to create something that would be both adventurous and expressive.

'I have it so completely in mind that it should not take long to put it into shape for you to see,' Goff wrote to the Fords in 1947. 'I believe it will be my best to date.'[11]

The spherical shape was achieved through a combination of low masonry walls made from coal bricks – punctuated by lumps of translucent glass, or culletts – and steel ribs that connect to a central 'mast'. These arched steel supports are known as Quonset ribs, after the prefabricated huts made by the US Navy during the Second World War. Goff got to know these huts well during his wartime service with the Seabees (Naval Construction Battalions), and used them to maximum effect here, where they are painted an orangey red, Ruth Ford's favourite colour.

The roof was coated in cedar shingles, and the ceilings finished in cypress boards, laid in a herringbone pattern, along with coiled rope for the ceilings in the lower portions of the house. The resulting dome is a very simple form, yet Goff took an ingenious approach to the internal plan, preserving the sense of an open volume, while also creating subtle distinctions between the various spaces of the house. Within the main body of the dome, he created an outer ring, holding a fluid sequence of living zones, and a sunken inner ring, which contains the kitchen. Integrated elements, including a curvaceous banquette around the fireplace,

Above An aerial view of the house shows the main dome, including the porch, which is partially protected by the red Quonset ribs.

Opposite Seen from the rear garden, the building also reveals two of its satellites to either side, with each holding a bedroom and bathroom.

Below A view from the entrance, showing the steel ribs of the dome, as well as the coiled rope used to coat the ceilings in the lower areas of the house.

Right The ingenious spatial planning provides an outer ring of living zones, and a two-tiered space with a sunken kitchen and mezzanine studio above.

help preserve a sense of order and cohesion, while fitted bookshelves double as partial partitions between the two rings. Goff added a mezzanine above the sunken core, offering a studio for Ruth Ford, toplit by a skylight that wraps around the central mast.

Adding to the spatial dexterity of the house, Goff reserved one large segment of the dome to serve as a porch, with a degree of shelter provided by the exposed Quonset ribs. The porch offers a seating area at ground level with its own fireplace, plus a balcony above overlooking the garden. Around the central dome, he then added three satellites – one holding the covered carport by the front door, and the others containing one bedroom and bathroom each.

Below The outer circle of the main dome holds a choice of spatial zones, including this seating area; the bedrooms sit in two satellites.

Opposite The semi-covered porch sits within one segment of the main dome, holding an outdoor fireplace at lower ground level and a balcony above.

In the manner of the organic approach adopted by Goff and advocated by his piecemeal mentor Frank Lloyd Wright (p. 54), Ford House has a strong relationship with its setting, even if it is essentially suburban. The house is rich in a range of organic textures, including the warm cypress boards and the jute ropework, as well as the coal and glass walls. The combination of an organic design philosophy, together with sculptural prowess and spatial dexterity, invites comparison with the Price Residence (p. 248), designed thirty years later by Goff's student Bart Prince, and commissioned by a shared client and key supporter of both architects.

Goff's individual, flexible building remains a home that is suited to both contemplative

pleasures and to the concerts and events that have been held here. For the last few decades, the house has been owned by another architect, Sidney K. Robinson, who has spoken of the 'profound stimulus' offered by his time living in a building that is grounded in simplicity, yet layered with complexity.

'It resonates on an astonishing range of references,' he wrote. 'The Ford House shows how the unconventional is not just a disruptive, avant-garde gesture; it is a hopeful way to expand daily life.'[12]

[11] David G. De Long, 'Bruce Goff's Ford House: Living in Joyful Order', in *Friends of Kebyar 30.3:82 (2015)*.
[12] Ibid.

Healy Guest House

SARASOTA, FLORIDA

Ralph Twitchell & Paul Rudolph (1950)

Regarded as the godfather of the Sarasota Modern style, Ralph Twitchell was an innovator who combined a passion for architecture with a solid understanding of the business of building. When he established his architectural practice in Sarasota, Florida, in 1931, he also opened a construction company (Associated Builders) and began exploring fresh tectonic ideas, moving away from the Mediterranean style of architecture that characterized some of his earliest residential projects and embracing modernity.

In 1941, Twitchell was joined by a younger architect, Paul Rudolph (p. 126), who had studied at Harvard under Walter Gropius (p. 48), the former head of the Bauhaus. Together, Twitchell and Rudolph designed a series of pioneering projects that served as the foundation for what became known as the Sarasota School of Architecture. These were residences that fused the key principles of Modernism – curtain walls, open-plan living spaces, inside–outside connectivity, linear forms, and so on – with an understanding of the subtropical climate and conditions of Florida.

One of the most influential of these projects was modest in scale, but large in impact – a guest house commissioned by Twitchell's parents-in-law, Mr and Mrs W.R. Healy, which was intended as a satellite to a larger residence that was never built. The site was a delight in itself, sitting towards the end of a private lane on the banks of a bayou on Bay Isle. Like many Sarasota neighbourhoods, it is a place that feels like a hinterland between land and sea.

The Healy Guest House is just 71 m² (760 sq ft) in size, arranged on one level, with two small bedrooms and a bathroom, yet manages to explore a multitude of ideas in a project the architects described as a 'tour de force'. They placed the cottage on the edge of the bayou, so that the sun deck, or balcony, cantilevers out over the water. The timber-framed, post-and-beam building was raised slightly above ground level on a series of supporting pillars, or pilotti. A small porch leads straight into a largely open-plan living space, with a kitchen by the front door that flows through to a combined living and dining area.

Above The house has the look of a lightweight pavilion, floating on the bayou, an impression enhanced by the way it rests on a series of pilotti.

Opposite Seen from across the water, the concave shape of the 'cocoon' roof can be appreciated, along with how the house balances openness and privacy.

Below Inside, the concave shape of the ceiling defines the character of the main living area, with the timber joinery warming and softening the interiors.

Opposite The retractable wall of glass at one end of the house offers an open view of the water, enhancing the sense of space and openness.

One cabin-style bedroom sits in a more or less central core, with the other at the far end of the cottage, next to a compact bathroom. The curtain-wall structure allows for a combination of floor-to-ceiling glass – both fixed and sliding – and jalousie windows that offer shade and natural cross-ventilation.

Yet the most innovative element of the cottage – or 'Cocoon House', as it is sometimes known – was the roof. During his military service with the US Navy during the Second World War, Rudolph had noted how the more delicate portions of warships, such as gun turrets, were mothballed using a system of wire frames sprayed with a polymer

of thin, plastic Saran wrap (produced by the Dow Chemical company) and vinyl. This created a protective and watertight 'cocoon' that the architects suggested could last thirty years or more.

Twitchell and Rudolph designed a concave roof using a series of steel supporting straps, sprayed with the polymer. The structure and shape of the roof was carefully engineered to allow rainwater to drain away, but allow the cocoon to expand and contract in the heat without causing damage to the rest of the house and the glasswork, in particular. Just as importantly, the roof has the feel of a gentle wave that softens the linear outline

The two modest bedrooms have the feel of ship's cabins, while jalousie windows help control the light and provide privacy from passing boats.

of the cottage, connecting it back to the water and the coast. This helps to create a more sculptural composition, as well as to preserve the essential modesty of the cottage, while the use of glazing, screens and a sun deck maximizes the relationship between house and the bayou.

'In a sense, this is an anti-social building, for it ignores the neighbouring assortment of non-committal houses,' wrote Twitchell and Rudolph. 'It can even be said that it dominates the bayou, because of its placement, form, colours and materials. The surrounding structures are already covered with a profusion of lush growth; in this cottage, however, we wanted to demonstrate that harmony between the work of nature and the work of man can be brought about by differentiating between the two.'[13]

The cottage is now leased by the Sarasota Architectural Foundation, who have sensitively restored the building in order to replicate the original design, with interiors and furnishings by designer Ellen Hanson.

[13] Ralph Twitchell and Paul Rudolph, 'Cocoon House', in *Architectural Forum*, January 1951.

Dawnridge

BEVERLY HILLS, CALIFORNIA

Tony Duquette & Caspar Ehmcke (1949)

Above The house and garden serve as a canvas for Duquette's sculptures and installations, often made with pieces of salvage and re-purposed elements.

Opposite Sitting within a lush hillside garden, the house extends outwards into its setting via a hinterland of terraces and outdoor rooms.

Tony Duquette was a master of many different media. As an interior designer, his clients included Doris Duke, J. Paul Getty, Mary Pickford and Elizabeth Arden, and as a furniture designer he created pieces for Elsie de Wolfe, among many other clients. He was also a sculptor, artist and jewelry designer, and had a successful career as a Hollywood set designer, working on films such as Yolanda and the Thief (1945), directed by Vincente Minnelli and starring Fred Astaire.

This combination of interiors and set design – for film and theatre – lends comparison with the work of contemporaries such as Oliver Messel and Lorenzo Mongiardino, who also traversed such borders with great success. Duquette's multi-layered interests and talents fused together seamlessly upon the canvas of his own homes, which became extraordinary laboratories, full of pattern, texture and colour, within his 'more is more' approach to design and aesthetics. These were, in themselves, pieces of theatre – full of life, vitality and the fruits of Duquette's endless hoarding and collecting.

'Until I was an adult, and then for nearly fifty happy years with my artist wife, I have gone on accumulating, like a fascinated magpie, enough beautiful things, ugly things, curious things – from deer's antlers to Siamese figures of gilded wood – to fill boxes and boxes, baskets and baskets, houses and houses,' he noted in a lecture entitled 'The Enchanted Vision'.[14]

One house – called Sortilegium, a fantasy world formed by a collage of salvage and ephemera, created by Duquette at his ranch in Malibu – was destroyed by fire in 1993. The house that survived, and still showcases his highly individual aesthetic, is Dawnridge in Beverly Hills. Here, Duquette worked with architect and occasional collaborator Caspar Ehmcke, a German émigré who became well known for his Hollywood homes. Together, they designed a new house that was modest in both plan and scale – at around 84 m² (900 sq ft) – but packed full of imagination and character.

The undulating hillside garden became an extension of the house itself, with loggias, terraces and garden rooms forming an exotic,

Above The sitting room is full of theatre; sunburst screens to either side of the doorway were made with car hubcaps and other everyday items.

Opposite Mirrors increase the illusory quality of the space, with a chandelier made with Venetian glass lilies and artworks by Duquette and his wife.

layered hinterland between inside and out. In the grounds, Duquette and his wife Elizabeth ('Beegle'), added a painting studio, a pavilion and a Thai-inspired guest house, creating a small compound of interrelated structures within the lush planting.

Despite the relatively modest scale of the main house, Duquette created a good deal of spatial and visual complexity within this highly individual retreat. The entrance hallway marks the transition from the streetscape and the elegant, symmetrical façade by introducing the first of many playful illusions and games, via a series of trompe-l'oeil murals, painted by Beegle, and the use of mirrors to further trick the eye and enhance the feeling of space.

The interiors have been restored by Duquette's business partner, Hutton Wilkinson, who now owns the house and continues to run the studio. The curated collection of designs includes a secretaire designed for Elsie de Wolfe and bespoke screens with a recurring starburst motif featuring re-purposed hubcaps.

Such recycling sat naturally within Duquette's love of illusion, which fused the precious and the everyday. Like a Piero Fornasetti interior, Dawnridge is a true original, full of drama and delight, where Duquette was in his element and the star of the show.

[14] Hutton Wilkinson, *More is More: Tony Duquette* (New York: Abrams, 2009).

Now glassed in, the garden room provides an extension of the living spaces, and an exuberant dining area backed with Duquette's signature 'malachite gemstone' wallcovering; the green sofa was originally designed for Doris Duke.

Eames House

PACIFIC PALISADES, CALIFORNIA

Charles & Ray Eames (1949)

Above The exterior features banks of glass, infills made from Cemesto boards and brightly coloured panels, creating a Mondrian-esque collage.

Opposite Over time, the line of eucalyptus trees has matured, forming a natural sun screen and softening the linear outline of the house.

For Charles and Ray Eames, there were no borders separating the world of art and design. They traversed any boundaries between the disciplines constantly, following their interests, passions and their imaginations. The Eameses are unique in the world of mid-century design in creating a portfolio of such depth and breadth, encompassing furniture and product design, graphics, photography, film-making, architecture and exhibitions.

The couple's creative process embraced communication in its broadest sense. This might mean a house, a toy, a chair or a film, all of which were concerned with transmitting fresh ideas with passion, originality, playfulness and intelligence. It was a philosophy that was commonplace at the Cranbrook Academy of Art in Michigan, a design school partly based on the Bauhaus model. Charles Eames served as head of the Industrial Design department, where he met a student called Ray Kaiser in 1940; they were married a year later. It would be one of the most important and productive collaborative relationships in the history of design.

Each brought complementary talents to the equation. Charles had trained and worked as an architect, but also had a long-standing passion for photography and the power of the visual image. Ray had studied painting for many years and was an accomplished artist, as well as a graphic designer and art director. Together, there was very little they couldn't do.

During the war years, the couple famously developed a lightweight, stackable leg splint for use by the US Navy, as well as a body stretcher, both made from plywood. Working in their Los Angeles apartment building (itself designed by Richard Neutra; p. 72), they continued to experiment with innovative materials, including fibreglass and wire mesh. Much of the furniture that they went on to develop over the following years has become iconic: warm, practical, friendly, affordable, versatile, comfortable and unpretentious.

When it came to building a house for themselves in Pacific Palisades, on a hilltop site overlooking the ocean, the design was – once again – both collaborative and pioneering. The combined home and studio

Below The studio, set slightly apart from the main house, is largely double-height, with a mezzanine level accessed by a simple steel stairway.

Opposite The double-height living room is at the far end of the house; in the central section, the kitchen is at ground level and the bedrooms above.

was built using prefabricated components, yet it also was dynamic in its layout and use of colour and texture, imbued with a sense of warmth and character, as well as modernity. The house was one of the brightest exemplars of the Case Study programme, a highly influential series of experimental homes published in *Arts & Architecture* magazine, whose editor, John Entenza, was a friend of the couple. Ray Eames had also designed a number of covers for the magazine. Entenza's own house (Case Study #9), designed by Charles Eames and Eero Saarinen (p. 120), was next door, and shared the same parcel of land.

The steel framework was erected in just a day and a half, with a courtyard providing a modest degree of separation between work and home. The two-storey structure was coated in a linear lattice of glazing, Cemesto boards and brightly coloured panels, arranged in an abstract formation that was somewhat reminiscent of the work of Piet Mondrian and his De Stijl contemporaries. At the far end, furthest from the studio, the rear wall and roofline projected outwards to shelter the veranda, while a line of eucalyptus trees ran parallel to the house, helping to provide shelter and shade.

Inside, the house offers striking contrasts between soaring, open spaces, such as the double-height living room, and more modest, intimate retreats like the bedrooms. The original interiors suggested a strong

Above The stairway in the studio has the look and feel of a ship's ladder, while the spiral staircase in the main house has a more sculptural quality.

Opposite The sitting room features a wall of books to the rear and a number of furniture designs by the couple; it leads out to a partially shaded terrace.

Japanese influence, including the use of tatami mats in the main living area, yet the spaces evolved many times over the years, with the introduction of additional furniture and collected treasures. The studio itself is partially double-height, but also features a mezzanine level.

The studio and house became a lifelong laboratory, a focal point for a busy and accomplished working life, where the creative process never stopped. Charles Eames extended his love of photography into film, using the medium as an educational and inspirational tool, as with films such as *Day of the Dead* (1957) and *Powers of Ten* (1968), a mesmerizing study of scale and perspective. Every year offered a wave of new projects, each very different from the last and from one other. Charles and Ray Eames always lived life to the full, making the most of all the opportunities open to them. It was this, as much as the work itself, which makes them such an inspiration.

Glass House

NEW CANAAN, CONNECTICUT

Philip Johnson (1949)

Philip Johnson described his New Canaan estate as the 'diary of an eccentric architect'. In 1946 he had bought just over five acres of land here and – along with his partner, curator and collector David Whitney – added to the property over the decades, eventually acquiring a total of forty-seven acres. The bucolic landscape was gradually punctuated by a series of structures that embodied, as Johnson put it, the 'chameleon-like quickness of my changes of approach to the art of architecture'.[15]

In time, this 'diary' would embrace a semi-subterranean painting gallery (1965), a sculpture gallery (1970), and a library/study in the postmodern style (1980), as well as a series of playful follies. But the most famous building was, of course, the Glass House, completed in 1949. Sitting on the brow of a hill, on a spot that Johnson identified when he first walked his initial plot of land, it is a pavilion for viewing the extraordinary landscape. The steel-framed house, with its flat roof and glass walls, is a modernist belvedere for appreciating the natural world and the changing seasons.

Essentially, the Glass House is a single room, or universal space. The only exception is a circular brick drum, floating within the crisp rectangle, which holds a small bathroom and a fireplace facing the main seating area. The rest of the house is defined by Johnson's careful placement of the furniture, with the seating area at the centre, facing an open vista, flanked by a dining area and bar/kitchenette to one side and a bedroom/study to the other, which is lent a degree of privacy by the presence of the drum and a half-height wardrobe sitting on the herringbone brick floor. Each element in the space is curated and controlled, including a painting on an easel by Nicolas Poussin and a sculpture by Elie Nadelman.

The house owes much to the work of the pioneering Bauhaus master, Ludwig Mies van der Rohe. Johnson had known of Mies's work since the 1920s, and had championed him in America. After Mies's arrival in the US in the 1930s, Johnson became an occasional associate, with the two architects famously collaborating on the design of the Seagram Building (1958) in New York.

Above The house looks out across a natural dip in the landscape, while a significant portion of the estate is blanketed in woodland.

Opposite The single-storey, steel-framed belvedere is largely transparent, allowing the landscape to filter through the building.

The open and universal space within the house is divided into zones by the arrangement of the furniture, including designs by Mies van der Rohe.

The Glass House is clearly indebted to the design of Farnsworth House (p. 108), designed by Mies, which was completed a year or so later to a design known to Johnson. Much of the furniture in the house is also by Mies, some of which was transferred over from Johnson's apartment in New York.

But this debt does not detract from its timeless beauty and powerful relationship with its surroundings, or from the purity of its execution. Johnson brought much to the project, including the Brick House, which sits discreetly nearby. While the Glass House is completely open, its subservient twin is enigmatic and closed, with very few windows and apertures. It acted as a service satellite and guest house, allowing the main house to retain its own clear purpose and character.

The twin houses also helped inform what can be seen as a golden period in Johnson's own architectural career, which spanned the 1950s and included some truly original homes, including Leonhardt House (1956) in Lloyd Neck, New York, and Wiley House (1953), also in New Canaan. Johnson left the estate to the National Trust for Historic Preservation, and it is open to visitors.

[15] David Whitney and Jeffrey Kipnis (eds), *Philip Johnson: The Glass House* (New York: Pantheon Books, 1993).

Below The brick drum holds the fireplace and a bathroom; a bank of cupboards provides some privacy for the sleeping zone and study beyond.

Opposite The kitchenette is a minimal installation; the Brick House nearby offers more in the way of service spaces and guest accommodation.

Farnsworth House

PLANO, ILLINOIS
Ludwig Mies van der Rohe (1951)

Dr Edith Farnsworth was an unlikely revolutionary. She studied English Literature at the University of Chicago, and followed her passion for music at the American Conservatory of Music and in Rome during the 1920s. Having fallen in love with Italy, its music and literature, she returned to the country in the 1960s and translated the work of the poet Eugenio Montale and others. Farnsworth also fell in love, more or less, with one of the greatest architects of the 20th century, and commissioned one of his most radical and influential buildings.

Farnsworth studied medicine at Northwestern University during the 1930s, eventually becoming a Chicago-based kidney specialist. In the mid-1940s she met Ludwig Mies van der Rohe, a former director of the Bauhaus, who had emigrated to America, assumed the directorship of the Armour Institute and launched a second career with a new practice in Chicago. By this time, Mies was in a relationship with the sculptor Lora Marx, but this did not stop an infatuation developing between the architect and his new client.

Farnsworth asked for a modest weekend and vacation home near Plano, Illinois, around 100 km (60 miles) away from Chicago, and next to the Fox River. Given Mies's reputation, it is not surprising that she offered her architect something close to carte blanche when it came to designing her new home. Certainly, Mies seized the opportunity to create something truly revolutionary, which offered nothing less than a new way of living.

Mies designed a rectangular steel-framed house, raising it above the meadow to help reduce the risk of flooding. This gives the building a sense of lightness, with its crisp form seeming to float above the ground – a sensation reinforced by the house's transparency, with its curtain walls of floor-to-ceiling glass, which allow an immediate sense of connection with the landscape and the surrounding trees. The vibrant synergy between inside and out is further enhanced by the open veranda at one end, and the adjoining terrace, positioned almost in parallel with the house and just a few steps lower, yet still above the ground plane.

Above Concerns about flooding led to the house being elevated on pilotti, although it has nevertheless been damaged by floods over the years.

Opposite Floor-to-ceiling glass allows the landscape to be an integral part of the house; the terrace further dissolves boundaries between inside and out.

Within the universal space of the house, the architect zoned areas for seating and working through the placement of furniture; the core to the right holds the fireplace, service spaces and a galley kitchen.

The outline and composition of Farnsworth House were radical enough for the times, with Mies drawing on the structural and spatial ideas he developed for the Barcelona Pavilion (1929) and Tugendhat House (1930) in Brno, in the Czech Republic, both of which made use of curtain walls and banks of glass. But here, on the meadow by the Fox River, Mies went further than ever before, creating a modern belvedere.

Mies continued the experiment within the house, effectively creating a universal space devoted to open-plan living. The house can be seen as one large room, with a service core towards the centre holding a galley kitchen to one side and a fireplace to the other, flanked by small, hidden bathrooms and services. Mies also intended it to be 'zoned' only by the arrangement of the furniture, with seating around the fireplace and a sleeping area tucked away behind a free-standing wardrobe at one end.

Despite starting a revolution, in design and architecture, Edith Farnsworth was not pleased, calling the house her 'Mies-conception'. The architect had

Opposite A floating wardrobe helps to lightly partition the sleeping area beyond; the majority of the furniture here was designed by the architect.

Below The original kitchen is compact and functional; the sleeping area is at the far end of the pavilion, close to a bathroom contained within the core.

underestimated the mosquitoes that plagued his client, to the point that she asked a friend to design screens around the porch, which were installed in 1952. Farnsworth found inhabiting such a transparent and unforgiving space a challenge, and complained: 'I can't even put a clothes hanger in my house without considering how it affects everything from the outside.'[16]

With any shared passion now on ice, architect and client fell out dramatically. They ended up in court, with Mies suing for unpaid fees and Farnsworth counter-suing for cost overruns and a leaking flat roof. Mies won the case, and the two never spoke again, with the ripples spilling out into their wider social circle. But, tellingly,

Edith Farnsworth never sold up. Apart from time in Italy during the 1960s, she kept her revolutionary home until the end. Today, it is a place of architectural homage.

[16] Maritz Vandenberg, *The Farnsworth House* (London: Phaidon, 2003).

Butterfly House

CARMEL, CALIFORNIA

Frank Wynkoop (1951)

Above Recent restoration has reinstated the kidney-shaped pool in the central courtyard; the sculpture by the entrance is by artist Peter Lane.

Opposite The 'butterfly' roof hovers above decks that surround the house and reinforce the maritime influences playing on the design of the building.

With its distinctive roofline and extraordinary setting, perched above Carmel Bay, the Butterfly House is a local landmark. More than this, it is a unique building with a romantic resonance that speaks of a postwar period full of optimism and ambition. It encapsulates the playful spirit of mid-century design and the dream of oceanside living, offering an immediate sense of connection to the ever-changing seascape.

Frank Wynkoop was a successful architect, based in Bakersfield and then San Francisco. His focus was largely on schools, but there were wartime housing projects. The Butterfly House is his only recorded one-off residence, designed for himself and his family. The spot he chose was inspired – not far from Clinton Walker House (1948) by Frank Lloyd Wright, the site pushes out into the bay, with the waves crashing on the rocks below. Today, mature trees help to soften the site, yet – as the architect appreciated – the greatest prize was the view of the ocean.

Wynkoop designed a steel-framed, single-storey building, with the 'butterfly' roof rising to meet the sea. The main living spaces are at this end of the house, with banks of glass facing the open vista, partially protected by the roofline. A balcony cantilevers out over the rocks like the prow of a ship, further enhancing the relationship with the coastline.

The positioning of the house left it and its residents exposed to the elements, so Wynkoop also created a large courtyard, complete with a swimming pool and terracing around it. In the original plan for the house, the courtyard was to double as a circulation space, creating constant connectivity with the outside. Four bedrooms sat to one side of this courtyard, with service spaces and a lanai (an open-sided veranda) at the other.

Wynkoop embedded the house into the landscape, balancing bricks for solidity with banks of glass for transparency and light. Old photos of the living room and its circular fireplace suggest the feel of a ship's bridge for this part of the house, with the curving lines of pieces such as the sectional settee echoing the waves. The architect also added a modest upper storey, which held an additional bedroom, reminiscent of an elevated lookout post.

Below The main living area flows out towards the pool terrace and central courtyard; the feature wall at the far end is by artist Stan Bitters.

Opposite The curving lines of the pool help to soften the house, while the courtyard acts as a generous outdoor room, sheltered from the sea breezes.

Sadly, it seems as though the $100,000-plus cost of building the house may have been a factor in Wynkoop's decision to sell it just five years later. It was in the hands of another owner for around fifty years, followed by a renovation that stripped away a number of key features, including the kidney-shaped swimming pool and parts of the courtyard terrace.

More recently, the current owners asked interior designer Jamie Bush to restore the house's essential mid-century character. He exposed the original steel beams, adopted a warm, textural palette, and designed many integrated elements, echoing the wave-like shapes seen in Wynkoop's original plans. The restoration seems fully in keeping with the house's original playful spirit.

'We really wanted to bring the rugged, textural landscape into the house, so that it felt married to the place and rooted in a naturalistic, Northern Californian aesthetic of materiality,' Bush says. 'There are a lot of built-ins and everything is very crafted and handmade, as you might see on a boat. It's something that has been made to last long after we are gone.'[17]

[17] Interview with the author.

Opposite A sunken seating area offers a viewing point for appreciating the ocean and the coastline.

Below The sea provides a constant and ever-changing backdrop to the main living area; the matching armchairs are by Sergio Rodrigues.

Miller House

COLUMBUS, INDIANA
Eero Saarinen (1957)

Industrialist and philanthropist J. Irwin Miller was one of the great supporters of mid-century architecture. After studying at Yale and Oxford, he joined the family business, overseeing its dramatic expansion in the field of commercial diesel engines. Among other posts, he became chairman of the Irwin Union Bank in Columbus and served as president of the National Council of Churches.

From the late 1930s, Miller played a key role in commissioning and promoting modern architecture in the small city of Columbus, Indiana. The Cummins Foundation, which he founded, helped to fund a whole range of new buildings, creating an extraordinary portfolio that includes work by I.M. Pei, César Pelli, Robert Venturi (p. 168) and Richard Meier (p. 230), yet Miller's first architectural loyalty was to Eero Saarinen.

Saarinen first began working in Columbus when he assisted his father, Eliel Saarinen (p. 36), with the design of the First Christian Church (1939). Later, he designed a bank for Irwin Union in 1955, followed by the North Christian Church in 1963, with its dramatic roofline topped by a pencil-point spire. He

was also entrusted with the design of Miller's family home, which became the architect's most accomplished residential commission.

The site has a semi-rural quality, sitting within extensive grounds designed by Dan Kiley. The house, a spacious single-storey, flat-roofed pavilion of steel and glass, accessed via long processional entry sequence, sits on a neat plateau overlooking a sunken meadow. The roof canopy extends outwards, helping to shelter a series of terraces around the building, which blur the boundaries between inside and out.

Inside, Saarinen created a quartet of rectangular sub-pavilions in each corner. Each of these units has its own clear purpose and identity, with one holding the kitchen and service spaces and another a guest suite. The sub-pavilions on the other side of the house contain the children's bedrooms and a playroom, which later became Xenia Miller's study, and the master suite, with space for two dressing rooms and another study. The more central area between these four blocks serves as a fluid living space, divided into various zones.

Above The overhanging roof forms a canopy that helps protect the terraces, which serve as a hinterland between the interiors and the gardens.

Opposite This part of the house holds sheltered garaging and the main entrance; the internal spaces beyond originally served as guest quarters.

The central portion of the house is open
and fluid, including the dining area,
the main sitting room and – beyond the
piano – a den.

At the heart of this universal space is a
seating area arranged around a circular
fireplace; another is in a welcoming
conversation pit. A dining area sits to one
side, with a den to the other, and curtains
that can be pulled across to separate the
two zones. The internal walls are covered
in marble, and a series of carefully positioned
skylights add further natural light.

There is fitted furniture, plenty of storage
and a long library wall running from the
fireside seating area into the den. Saarinen's
'Tulip' table and chairs grace the dining area;
elsewhere are pieces by George Nelson,
Carlo Scarpa, Charles and Ray Eames (p. 96)
and Alexander Girard, who collaborated on
the interior design. His work adds colour,
texture and playful touches, including
'shadow boxes' peopled with Mexican
and South American maquettes.

The setting, architecture and interiors
work together to make this one of the most
delightful of mid-century American homes.
Left by the family to the Indianapolis Museum
of Art, the house retains most of its original
detailing, and is open to the public.

Below The large, colourful kitchen offers a picturesque view of the gardens designed by Dan Kiley.

Opposite The interiors were designed with Alexander Girard, who played an important part in layering the house with colour and character.

Umbrella House

SARASOTA, FLORIDA

Paul Rudolph (1953)

During the 1950s and '60s, the residential roofscape was revisited and reinvented. Far from being a simple, binary choice between pitched or flat, rooflines became an increasingly important component part of the structural and tectonic approach, as well as a more expressive element within the composition as a whole. Architects often regarded the roof as something that could become dynamic and sculptural.

Paul Rudolph began exploring innovative structural solutions during his partnership with Sarasota architect Ralph Twitchell. One of their most important joint projects, the Healy Guest House, or 'Cocoon House' (1950; p. 84), was lifted well above the ordinary by, in large part, its extraordinary concave roof. Another design, the Coward Residence (1951), was constructed as a sequence of complementary structures with tent-like roofs, creating a variation of the earlier 'catenary cocoon' system.

After forming his own practice in Sarasota in 1951, Rudolph continued to innovate. Hook Guest House in Siesta Key, Florida, completed in 1952, featured a triple-vaulted roof that lent the house a rhythmic, wave-like form. A year later, Umbrella House was completed, in which the roof – or canopy – was also the defining feature.

Also known as the Hiss Residence, the house was commissioned by property developer and entrepreneur Philip Hiss. A great supporter and advocate of modern architecture, Hiss worked closely with Rudolph and Tim Seibert, who worked initially in Rudolph's office, before becoming an in-house architect for Hiss, for whom he designed, among other projects, the distinctive Hiss Studio (1953), another Sarasota landmark.

When he first approached Rudolph, Hiss was in the early days of working on his Lido Shores housing development, situated on a spur of land between St Armands Key and Longboat Key, and forming part of the barrier island chain between Sarasota Bay and the Gulf of Mexico. Hiss wanted to create a bold and distinctive new house on a prominent site just off John Ringling Parkway, which would attract attention to the new development.

Above The roof canopy extends outwards to cover the terrace, with an opening at the centre of the 'umbrella' above the swimming pool.

Opposite The façade of the two-storey house has a strong, linear quality, while the canopy helps to shelter a vast porch around the entrance.

Opposite A secondary lounge sits to one side, arranged around a fireplace and tucked beneath a mezzanine gallery, linking the bedrooms.

Below The main seating area filters out to the pool terrace via glass doors; the choice of mid-century furniture is sympathetic to the period of the house.

For his client, Rudolph created a sophisticated, rectangular house with a dramatic double-height, open-plan living area at the centre, and ancillary spaces and bedrooms arranged over two storeys at either end. A mezzanine gallery overlooking the living room helped to connect the bedrooms upstairs. The living area was lightly zoned yet fluid, with a more intimate sunken seating area tucked beneath the mezzanine and arranged around a fireplace, with the rest of the space used for dining and entertaining.

Rudolph's grand gesture was to create a canopy, or 'umbrella', which floats above this linear pavilion, extending outwards to encompass the terraces around the swimming pool. This secondary roof serves as a vast, slatted brise soleil, providing shade for the house and the outdoor room arranged around the central pool, where it is punctured to allow a view of the sky. The shading system mitigated any potential glasshouse effect from the large banks of windows and glass doors at the back of the house, facing the pool and garden.

Below The canopy also helps to shade and protect the bedrooms on the upper level, while the louvred glass windows offer natural ventilation.

Opposite A sub-canopy below the main umbrella underlines the strict geometry of horizontal and vertical lines that characterize the house.

Original and delightful, the Umbrella House instantly caught the public's attention, attracting visitors to the Lido Shores development and bringing fresh admiration for Rudolph's work. The house was widely published and well reviewed, further enhancing the architect's reputation as both an innovator and an influencer. Rudolph went to explore the idea of an integrated brise soleil at the Milam Residence (1961) in Jacksonville, which marked one of his last Florida projects, before his focus shifted to Yale University in Connecticut and New York.

The house was badly damaged during a tropical storm in the 1960s, when the 'umbrella' broke away. In 2011 new owners commissioned architect Greg Hall to undertake a full renovation of the house, which included the restoration of the canopy. Umbrella House can now be seen much as architect and client first intended.

Firestone House

RANCHO MIRAGE, CALIFORNIA

William Pereira (1957)

Above The house offers a balancing act between openness and privacy via a series of partially sheltered terraces and outdoor rooms.

Opposite The dramatic *promenade architecturale* includes a long porch with a roof canopy, bordered by slumpstone walls.

As an entrepreneur and philanthropist, Leonard Firestone was not content to simply run the tyre firm that gave his family its fortune. He served as president of the Firestone Tire & Rubber Company for many years, as well as ambassador to Belgium under Richard Nixon and Gerald Ford, founded a winery in Santa Ynez, California, and co-founded the Betty Ford Center. He also commissioned an extraordinary home in Rancho Mirage, designed by William Pereira and completed in 1957.

The Firestone estate, recently restored and updated, sits within three acres of grounds on the edge of the Thunderbird Country Club and its golf course. The San Jacinto mountains form a dramatic backdrop here in the Coachella Valley, while Palm Springs – where Pereira designed both the J.W. Robinson Department Store (1958) and the Convention Center (1974) – is just a few miles down the road.

Pereira is best known for landmark statements, including the Transamerica Pyramid (1972) in San Francisco and the sci-fi inspired Geisel Library (1970) at the University of California San Diego. Yet this home in the desert suggests that he was also a masterful residential architect, creating a quiet and contextual home in response to the natural beauty of the surroundings.

The front elevation is relatively enclosed, featuring high walls of slumpstone (a kind of characterful concrete brick), surrounding a secluded parking forecourt. The entrance is pushed deep into the overall outline of the house, creating a dramatic, processional sequence when stepping from the sunshine into an extended, sheltered porch, and then into the main house. Here, Pereira explores a series of relationships between inside and out, constantly blurring the line between them and connecting with the gardens and the landscape.

Pereira achieves this through multiple means, while always keeping privacy, as well as openness, in mind. There are relatively guarded courtyard spaces around the swimming pool and key bedrooms, which offer oases away from the golf links, yet also act as verdant outdoor rooms, with their own planting and sculpted trees providing

The main living space offers a vivid sense
of connection with the surrounding
gardens; furniture includes a mix of
bespoke pieces by Sam Cardella and
mid-century designs.

a welcome degree of shade. The dining
room and a semi-sheltered sun lounge
overlook the pool court, which is bordered
by a generous terrace, while sandstone
floors carry through from inside to outdoors.

There is also a managed degree of
crossover between interior and exterior
space towards the rear of the building,
where it looks out across the open greenery
of the golf course. Here, verandas form a
kind of hinterland, while providing additional
fresh-air living spaces. Low planters and a
water pool create a subtle boundary around
the private realm, without interrupting the
views through the floor-to-ceiling windows
from the main sitting room.

New owners have recently acquired the
house, and commissioned interior designer
Sam Cardella to undertake a sensitive and
thoughtful approach to the restoration of
the property, taking into account a number
of previous updates and minor alterations.
They inherited the original blueprints to
the main house, plus the semi-separate
guest house. Over the course of eighteen
months, Cardella worked on subtle changes

Opposite In the dining room, the chairs are vintage Knoll designs by Mies van der Rohe, apart from those at each end of the table, which date from the 1970s.

Below Many of the key living spaces, including the dining room and kitchen, look onto the secluded pool court and connect with it via walls of glass.

that enhance the experience of daily living at the house, while preserving its essential character and integrity.

One of the key challenges was the restoration of the banks of glazing; many of the steel-framed sliding windows, 3 m (10 ft) high, had seized up over the years and needed replacing. Services were also updated, and Cardella remodelled the master bedroom and bathroom to create a more welcoming and fluid suite of spaces. Many of the original integrated features designed by Pereira were carefully preserved, such as the fitted bar in the dining room and the focal point fireplace in the sitting room.

The curated blend of loose furniture not only includes custom pieces by Cardella and contemporary designs, but also a significant selection of mid-century and other vintage pieces. The extensive gardens were revived by landscape designer Marcello Villano, who stripped away the overgrowth while replanting in places, adding mature palms, cypress trees and a number of additional olive trees to complement the many original plants that remained in the grounds.

Frank House

FIRE ISLAND, NEW YORK
Andrew Geller (1958)

An endearing spirit of playful postwar optimism runs through the eighty or so holiday and beachside homes designed by Andrew Geller on Long Island, New York. They were modest and affordable, often built for less than $10,000, and generally made from timber. But they were also full of imagination and creativity, adopting sculptural shapes and idiosyncratic forms, like pieces of land art sited on the coastal landscape. The architect often gave these houses nicknames, including 'The Milk Carton', 'The Cat', 'The Gull', 'Box Kite' and 'The Grasshopper'.

The first in the long sequence of these characterful homes was a house at Sagaponack for Betty Reese. Geller and Reese were friends and colleagues at the New York office of Raymond Loewy Associates, where Geller was the head of the architecture department and Reese was the director of public relations. She asked her former colleague if he would be willing to design and build a small vacation home for her, with a budget of around $7,000, and he obliged.

The resulting home is a version of an A-frame cabin, with a loft-like master bedroom up in the roof, hovering above the main living spaces below and accessible via a retractable ladder. The house had charm and wit, and the delighted Reese fed the cabin into her own publicity machine. Soon Geller found himself with a second, parallel career designing houses on Long Island.

During the mid-1950s, Geller's houses caught the attention of Rudolph Frank, the owner of a Queens ice-cream company, and his wife Trudy, an artist and fashion illustrator. The couple had recently taken a vacation on the Yucatán peninsula in Mexico and had admired the Mayan temples they had seen on their travels. On showing their holiday photos to their architect, they asked if he could bring a touch of the Maya to the dunes at Fire Island Pines, a hamlet situated on one of the barrier islands floating off the southern coast of Long Island.

Nicknamed 'The Cube', Frank House does have a Mayan shape to it, as it peeks over the surrounding trees and scrub, seeking out a view of the sea. Rather than using stone,

Above The outline of the house suggests something of its Mayan inspiration; the pool is a more recent addition.

Opposite Multiple stairs and access points include the fireman's ladder at the front of the house and a spiral stairway winding up to the roof terrace.

Below The Larson Paul-designed kitchen includes furniture and lighting designs by Alvar Aalto and George Nelson, among others.

Opposite The main living area sits within a dramatic double-height space, with a bridge connecting the fireman's ladder to the bedrooms at mid-level.

Geller created the lightweight, two-storey house from timber, resting it just above the dunes on a series of wooden piles. The heart of the home is a double-height living space, with tall banks of glass looking onto the landscape and feeding out to a deck beyond. A fireman's ladder sits at the centre of the façade, meeting an elevated door and walkway spanning the void of the living space area and connecting with the master bedroom on the upper level. The flat roof above offers an extraordinary vantage point for looking out across Fire Island.

In July 1961, the house was featured in the pages of *Life* magazine, but over the ensuing years, the salt air and sometimes

challenging conditions of the island had taken their toll on the building, which, like its dwindling cousins, was designed initially to last just a few decades. A new owner, artist Philip Monaghan, commissioned architects Larson Paul to undertake a sensitive restoration, which began with re-supporting the house from below, and carried through into a meticulous process of updating that respected the house's original character.

A new deck and swimming pool were added at the front of the house, enhancing the charm of one of Geller's most delightful commissions. Cladding and glazing were also upgraded. Inside, the position of the guest bedroom and kitchen on the ground

Opposite The sitting room from the mezzanine, with its wood-burning stove and comfortable seating; a wall of glass brings the trees right into the house.

Below The sense of space and volume can be fully appreciated from the mezzanine; the modest bedrooms have the feel of ship's cabins.

floor were swapped to allow a more direct sense of connection between the new kitchen and the living area. A wooden sliding door separates these two spaces from one another, as needed. Monaghan's choice of furniture and lighting is also highly sympathetic to the mid-century period, while the extensive use of timber inside and out – along with the vivid green backdrop offered by the setting – provides the house with a warm, organic quality.

Before his death in 2011, Geller visited the house and declared himself 'thrilled' with the restoration. It has given fresh life and vibrancy to one of the architect's most engaging houses at a time when the Geller portfolio of Long Island dream homes had shrunk over the years to perhaps a quarter of the original total.

Nakashima Farmstead & Conoid Studio

NEW HOPE, PENNSYLVANIA

George Nakashima (1959)

The woodworker and 'designer craftsman' George Nakashima treated his farmstead in Pennsylvania as a kind of laboratory, immersed in nature. Eventually growing to around ten acres, it was home to his workshops and lumber stores, all essential to the creation of his unique approach to furniture design, which established him as one of the most original voices in mid-century design.

'I would find it impossible to try to design a chair out of plastic or metal or plywood,' he said. 'But I do feel that in order to produce a fine piece of furniture, the spirit of a tree lives on and I can give it a second life … That's my objective and that's my happiness.'[18]

The farmstead was also a place where Nakashima was able to revisit his first career as an architect. From 1947 to around 1975, he designed a whole series of innovative buildings, fusing influences from both America and Japan, where he worked for a number of years with his mentor, Antonin Raymond. In 1943, Raymond sponsored the release of Nakashima and his family from an internment camp during the Second World

War. He had a farm in New Hope and offered Nakashima a job as a farmhand, but with enough time free to also make some of his early pieces of furniture.

After the war, Nakashima rented a cottage nearby, where he continued making furniture. A meeting with Hans Knoll led to an arrangement to produce a small collection for Knoll's company and, when Nakashima found a parcel of land nearby, he persuaded the landowner to grant him three acres, which he committed to paying off in the years that followed.

Having trained as an architect at the University of Washington and at MIT, Nakashima began to create the first in a collection of buildings that would grow to include around a dozen larger structures and storage sheds, plus smaller satellite buildings. One of the first was a workshop and studio, constructed while the family camped out on the farmstead. This was followed by a home for the Nakashimas and their two children, which was completed in around 1947 and positioned on the brow of a hill, looking down and across the sloping landscape.

Above Three views of the studio, with its distinctive shell roof. The building is pushed into the hillside, with the lower level devoted to storage.

Opposite The studio is one of the largest and most dramatic structures on the farmstead, which became a rural laboratory of design.

145

Below The main entrance to the studio; the distinctive outline of the roof can be glimpsed, along with a kitchenette to the rear.

Right The sinuous roofline creates a double-height space to the front, with framed views across the treetops; this part of the studio serves as a gallery.

A furniture showroom followed and, in 1959, the Conoid Studio, one of the most adventurous buildings, was completed. The studio was an opportunity for Nakashima to explore his love of shell structures, drawing inspiration from the work of the Mexican pioneer, Felix Candela. It is sheltered by a soaring concrete roof, sealed inside and out with additional protective coatings. This sculptural roofline covered a largely open-plan studio. The timber floors, paper window screens and Noguchi lanterns give the space a highly organic feel, and act as a foil to the concrete roof. A number of sculptures by Harry Bertoia, a friend of the family, can be seen here and elsewhere on the farm. An office, kitchenette and bathroom were

Opposite In the guest house, the comfortable central living room has a strong Japanese influence; the day bed can be used for seating or sleeping.

Below The luxurious bathroom is a delightful surprise, featuring a large tub inlaid with the names of Nakashima's family.

placed to the rear, so that the studio could also be used by family and guests, while a basement level was used as extra storage for Nakashima's growing 'library' of timber.

In 1975 he completed the Guest House, which sits alongside the family home and was also designed with a blend of Japanese and American influences. It features a universal space for sleeping, eating and relaxing, with a galley kitchen tucked neatly away behind a sliding *shoji* screen, and a serene 'Japanese Room' for contemplation or additional sleeping space. A sculptural tub in the bathroom is inscribed with the names of Nakashima's children and grandchildren.

His daughter Mira, an architect and designer herself, continues to run Nakashima Woodworkers. She collaborated with her father on a number of projects before his death in 1990.

'I love the Conoid Studio especially, which is where our design studio is,' she says. 'You get a real sense of what's going on outside, which is what traditional Japanese architecture is all about. You keep hold of the outside as part of your scenery when you are inside.'[19]

[18] Interview with George Nakashima, nakashimawoodworkers.com.
[19] Interview with the author.

Dragon Rock

GARRISON, NEW YORK

Russel Wright & David Leavitt (1961)

Above The house and studio have a respectful relationship with their surroundings, following the principles of organic architecture and design.

Opposite From the studio, it is possible to see how the main house is tied to the landscape and adapts to the shifting topography.

The multi-talented Russel Wright was one of the first celebrity designers, turning his hand to furniture, interiors, cutlery, textiles and, most famously, ceramics. His distinctive 'American Modern' dinner range in rich, organic colours was an extraordinary bestseller, with around 250 million pieces sold in the 1940s and '50s. His wife Mary helped to publicize and promote his work, and together they wrote another bestseller, a lifestyle manual called *Guide for Easier Living*, in 1950.

The Wrights already had a converted coach house in New York, when, in 1942, they bought seventy-five acres of land around an abandoned quarry near Garrison, a few hours' drive north of Manhattan, where they hoped to create an escapist retreat – a bucolic haven tied to the rugged landscape. This was Manitoga, an Algonquin word meaning 'place of the great spirit'.

Wright began restoring the woodlands, creating a network of pathways and diverting a stream into the old quarry to create a pond. But good fortune turned its back on the couple when Mary died of cancer tragically young, leaving Wright with a two-year-old daughter. He decided to push on with the dream of building a home at Manitoga, planning his designs from a small cabin on the estate. He worked out in precise detail how he wanted the house and studio to function and to look, sharing his ideas with architect David Leavitt. Above all, Wright wanted a home that respected the landscape he loved, while connecting with it as directly and intimately as possible.

'The house should complement this tiny part of the world,' he wrote in an essay about Manitoga. 'We should all try to preserve its beauty and be careful not to injure or desecrate it. More than this, we wish to demonstrate and enhance its natural beauty and charm. Expression of the particular use to which the house shall be put is important. The house is to be occupied by me and my daughter, both of whom have a great love of nature. While in it, we want to express our love of this land.'[20]

The extraordinary hillside site overlooks a quarry pool, surrounded by woodland. Pushed right into the hillside itself, the

Below A cedar tree trunk forms an axial point for the staircase, which winds from the sitting room to the dining area and kitchen below.

Opposite On the lowest level, the custom kitchen has an integrated serving counter that connects it with the dining area alongside.

house is arranged over a total of eleven different interconnected levels, with granite boulders from the site worked into the fabric of the walls and floors, and used to form the fireplace in the sitting room. The upper levels held two bedrooms for Wright's daughter and her nanny, with the lowest level containing a dining area and bespoke kitchen that opened onto a terrace.

The great trunk of a cedar tree emerged from the kitchen floor to form the main roof support of the house, while stone steps wound upwards alongside it to the central section of the building, which held the main living area and a mezzanine den. Here, Wright designed bespoke sofas and exotic wall panels in copper and laminated plastics, with plastered walls embedded

with pine needles for added texture. Sliding glass doors by the stone hearth opened onto another terrace, dissolving the boundary between inside and out.

The house was organic and respectful of nature, but it was also a laboratory of ideas. Wright experimented with materials and finishes, such as the sliding plastic doors in his daughter's bathroom, layered with butterflies. Here, the windows by the tub opened up completely, reinforcing that inside/outside relationship.

A little further up the hillside, Wright built a studio and guest pavilion for himself. Connected to the main house by a pergola walkway, the studio was a single-storey structure, topped by a green grass roof and infused with a strong Japanese influence.

Above The main seating area of the house is arranged around a corner fireplace, which appears to be set into the rocky hillside.

Opposite In the studio, a custom bookshelf forms a light separation between the sleeping area and Wright's private study beyond.

The designer used stones found on the site for door handles and coated the ceilings with burlap and epoxy resin, with leaves and pine needles added to the mix.

Apart from a separate guest bedroom and an enclosed bathroom, with views from the bathtub down into the woods and quarry pond, the studio was open plan, with bespoke furniture by Wright mixed with chair designs by George Nelson and Hans Wegner. A bespoke shelving unit in oak lightly separated Wright's desk and work zone from his bed. It was a perfect place for working, surrounded by nature. In recent years, the house and studio have been restored by the Russel Wright Design Center, who became custodians of the estate after Wright's death, and regularly open Manitoga to the public.

20 Russel Wright, et al, *Russel Wright: Good Design is for Everyone* (New York: Manitoga/Russel Wright Design Center, 2001).

Margaret Esherick House

PHILADELPHIA, PENNSYLVANIA

Louis Kahn (1961)

Architect Louis Kahn aimed for 'poetic monumentality' in his work. During the 1950s and '60s, he devoted himself increasingly to ambitious projects that fused modernity with the almost spiritual grace of the ancient temples and cathedrals he saw on travels around Europe in the 1920s. Kahn worked mostly in concrete and brick, yet his work was also characterized by extraordinary plays between light and dark, volume and mass, geometry and nature. There is a sculptural quality to many of his buildings, as though he shaped these vast structures by carving into their surfaces and planes.

There is also something of the monumental, and certainly of the poetic, about the small sequence of highly individual houses that Kahn designed in and around Philadelphia during the postwar period. Of these, one of the best known and most engaging is the Margaret Esherick House, located in the picturesque neighbourhood of Chestnut Hill on the northern edge of the city. Margaret Esherick, who owned a bookshop nearby, asked Kahn to design a home that would be fully tailored to her needs.

Her house was the very first to be built on the street, and looks onto a generous back garden bordered by trees, which help provide both shade and a degree of privacy from the neighbouring houses that arrived later. A marker on the rear terrace notes that the back of the building faces southeast, taking advantage of the sun, and the front faces northwest. Over the years, the trees have matured, softening the crisp, linear outline of the house.

The façade to the street is relatively enclosed, and the house only opens out to the garden as you step through the front door, pass through the hallway and arrive in the double-height living space that occupies around a third of the house. This 'great room' features two vast stacked picture windows looking onto the garden, with a fireplace forming a focal point to one side, enhanced by a tall slot window framing a view of the chimney beyond. To the front of the room is a wall of bookcases, topped by a rectangular window and punctuated by two thin shuttered apertures, which can be opened for natural cross-ventilation.

Above Although the house might appear largely symmetrical, nothing is quite as it first seems, within a constant and playful subversion of expectation.

Opposite A series of slots and shutters recall a finely tuned instrument that opens and closes according to the seasons and time of day.

Below The large dining-room window overlooks the garden and woodland beyond; the dining area sits within the two-storey portion of the house.

Right The double-height great room is a dramatic space with a feeling of openness and volume; the staircase is hidden behind the timber wall.

The staircase forms a spine separating the sitting room from the single-height dining room beyond, which is blessed with another large window facing the garden. Beyond this is a service wing, holding a sinuous, crafted timber kitchen made by Margaret's uncle, Wharton Esherick (p. 30). This compact kitchen is a work of art in itself, infused with ingenuity and space-saving elements, including a fold-out breakfast table.

The stairs lead up to a mezzanine landing, and then to the only bedroom in the house, separated from the landing by two pocket doors. The bedroom is spacious and dual-aspect, with integrated storage units tucked beneath the windows. The bathroom is

Above The great room features a library wall at one end; the one bedroom upstairs is spacious enough to double as a secondary lounge.

Opposite The beautifully crafted kitchen was designed by Wharton Esherick, and has been lovingly looked after by the current owners.

to one side, also with pocket doors. The bathroom has its own fireplace, while a push-in, pull-out sofa conceals a hidden bath.

Although the house appears largely symmetrical, nothing is quite as it seems. One end, with the 'floating' chimney flue, is symmetrical, yet the other is not, and the front façade has its own irregularities. The pathway leads to a recessed porch where the front door is set to one side, and the pattern of windows and shutters to either side of the porch is also unexpected, offering two mismatching T-shaped patterns set within the rendered façade. Looking at the rear elevation, the sequence is actually one of four unequal bays, with a degree of openness and enclosure to them.

All of this adds to the unique character of the house, which manages to subtly subvert expectations and geometry throughout in a way that is characteristic of Kahn's work. Here, the architect achieves his own version of poetic monumentality, yet, in terms of creating an inviting, playful home, the sense of proportion and scale – along with the relationship between inside and outside space – are also delightful.

Sadly, Margaret Esherick was able to enjoy her home for just a short period, succumbing to pneumonia at an early age in 1962. The house has recently been lightly restored and updated by owners, who have also furnished the interiors in a sympathetically manner.

Strick House

SANTA MONICA, CALIFORNIA
Oscar Niemeyer (1964)

Above Unlike the architect's typically curvaceous designs, the relatively linear house is softened by the gardens, terraces and outdoor rooms.

Opposite The design of the gardens drew inspiration from the work of Roberto Burle Marx, who often collaborated with Niemeyer.

Given his Communist sympathies, the relationship between the celebrated Brazilian architect Oscar Niemeyer and the United States was always going to be complex. He was, along with Le Corbusier, a key part of the design team of the United Nations Headquarters in New York, which was completed in 1952, but within a few years was barred from visiting the US on account of his political views and personal friendship with Fidel Castro.

In the 1960s, the film director, screenwriter and entrepreneur Joseph Strick visited Niemeyer's home in Rio de Janeiro, Canoas House (1954), along with the new capital Brasília, which featured many of the architect's most significant buildings. Strick asked Niemeyer to design a house for him in California, only to find that the latter would have to design it from a distance.

Client and architect communicated by post, as ideas for the house in Santa Monica developed and evolved, fuelled by photographs and topographical surveys. Anne Strick vetoed Niemeyer's first proposal, and the second – with its layer of subterranean bedrooms, rather like the Canoas House – was turned down by the planning authorities. The house that Strick finally decided to build was Niemeyer's third design – a linear, T-shaped building that made the most of connections between indoor and outdoor living spaces throughout.

The house was built by contractors who had worked on a number of the Case Study Houses in California, a programme initiated and promoted by magazine editor John Entenza. The principal portion of the building is open plan, offering a generously scaled and voluminous space that holds the living spaces, with the main seating area subtly distinguished from the dining area and kitchen by a shift in floor level. Banks of glass to either side connect with the gardens, while the adjoining crossbar of the house holds the bedrooms and service spaces.

Unfortunately for Strick, his marriage came to an end during construction, so it was only Anne and their two children who moved into the house when it was completed. The family lived in the house for the next forty years until it was sold to

Above Banks of glass offer a vivid relationship with the terrace and landscape beyond; the kitchen sits four steps up from the main sitting room.

Opposite The house serves as the perfect setting for Boyd's collection of mid-century furniture; the black stools and chairs are by Oscar Niemeyer.

a developer, who cleared the gardens with the intention of demolishing and replacing the building, until the local landmarks commission heard of the plans and blocked them. The story caught the attention of designer Michael Boyd, who seized the opportunity to buy the house and make the move from the East to the West Coast.

Respecting the provenance and character of the house, Boyd embarked on a sensitive programme of restoration. Beyond the introduction of modern services and amenities – as well as changes to some finishes, such as the new palmwood flooring in the main living space – the only significant alteration to the house's original fabric was the conversion and extension of the garage

on the lower ground floor, which became a spacious library. The gardens required more extensive restoration, with Boyd drawing inspiration from both Niemeyer and the landscape designer Roberto Burle Marx, with whom the architect had often collaborated. The restored house became the perfect backdrop for Boyd's extensive collection of mid-century furniture.

The restoration of the house won the approval of Niemeyer himself, although he was never able to visit his only completed residence in the US. For many years, Strick House never even appeared among listings of Niemeyer's projects, but this has since been rectified, and today it is recognized as an important part of the master's canon.

Opposite The former garage at lower ground level now serves as a two-storey library and study, full of books and featuring Hans Wegner's 'Ox' chair.

Below Seen from across the pool, the main living spaces have the look and feel of a semi-transparent glass pavilion, full of light.

Vanna Venturi House

PHILADELPHIA, PENNSYLVANIA

Robert Venturi (1964)

Above Venturi subtly subverts both symmetry and expectation throughout, seen in elements such as the off-centre chimney and irregular fenestration.

Opposite This characterful house is unlike anything else in its traditional neighbourhood, apart from Margaret Esherick House, just down the street.

The house that Robert Venturi designed for his mother in Chestnut Hill, on the northern outskirts of Philadelphia, is both inclusive and subversive. This is, in itself, apt for an architect and theorist who refused to be pigeon-holed or typecast, instead taking inspiration from the broad spectrum of history and architectural styles. Venturi was the great architectural magpie, gathering his treasures with intelligence and discernment, and putting them through the extraordinary filter of his own imagination.

His mother, Vanna, grew up in a relatively poor immigrant family in Philadelphia, before working for an interior-design firm and developing a passion for art and architecture. After the death of her husband, a fruit merchant, Vanna commissioned her son, who was by this time lecturing in architecture at the University of Pennsylvania, to design his first completed building, one that would be suited to her needs and new life.

'My mother's house was designed for her as an elderly window,' Venturi wrote, 'with her bedroom on the ground floor, no garage because she didn't drive, and room for a maid and possibly a nurse – and also, as appropriate, for her beautiful furniture, which I had grown up with. Otherwise, she did not make demands on the architect, her son, concerning its programme or its aesthetic – she was beautifully trusting.'[21]

The son seized his chance to create not just a home for his mother, but also a kind of manifesto that was to play an important part in defining his career and become a key marker in the evolution of Postmodernism. The house conveyed a design philosophy that was both thoughtful and fresh, and also remarkably rounded and considered. It is inclusive in that it draws freely and positively on so many different sources of inspiration. These include modernist and neoclassical points of reference, along with many familiar elements and characteristics derived from vernacular American residential architecture.

'It connects with ideas of mine of the time involving complexity and contradiction, of accommodation to its particular Chestnut Hill suburban context; to the aesthetic layering I learned from the Villa Savoye; its pedimented roof configuration, derived from the Low

Below Additional sunlight is drawn down into the main living area via the stairwell alongside; the 'Sheraton' chair is a design by the couple for Knoll.

Opposite The staircase wraps around the fireplace and forms a kind of buffer between the front entrance and main living spaces.

House of Bristol, Rhode Island; its split pediment, derived from the upper pediment of Blenheim Palace; the duality composition, derived from the Casa Girasole in Rome and involving explicit applied elements of ornament,' Venturi added. 'But it is a modern house; my mother enjoyed living in it and entertaining the many young architects who visited it.'[22]

But the house was also one of subversion. Like Louis Kahn, in whose Philadelphia office the young Venturi had worked for a time, the architect delighted in challenging expectations and conventions. Throughout its exterior form and composition, and within the interiors, Venturi plays a whole series of games with symmetry, proportion, volume,

scale and tradition. In this respect, the house follows the example of Kahn's own playful Margaret Esherick House (p. 156), which is just up the street and a short walk away, yet Venturi takes things much further.

From the outside, it appears – at first glance – possessed of a strong symmetrical outline. Yet looking more closely, one sees, for example, that the chimney is slightly off-centre, the entry porch is irregular and one side of the façade features a ribbon window and the other two square windows of different sizes.

Moving inside, the ground-floor living spaces are anchored around the combined assembly of the fireplace/chimney and the stairway that twists around it, with the stairs

Opposite The stairway, a physical embodiment of the twists and turns taken during the design of the house, doubles as an art gallery.

Below The upper storey, feeding out onto a small terrace, holds one of two bedrooms; multiple windows ensure a rich quality of light.

leading up to an additional bedroom on the upper level. But here again, the twist is essential, with neither the staircase nor the fireplace conforming to stereotypical patterns. All of the important elements of the American home are here – the hearth, the covered porch, the generous central living room – but they are subtly and consciously subverted and challenged.

This relatively modest, two-bedroom home manages to incorporate a rich breadth of thinking into one small building, arguably launching not only a career, but also a new architectural movement. It also sits within the mould of the classic parent–child

commission, a generous and creative gesture of encouragement comparable with, for instance, the home designed by Charles Gwathmey for his parents on Long Island (p. 204), built just one year later.

[21] Robert Venturi, *'Stories of Houses – Vanna Venturi House'*, www.storiesofhouses.blogspot.com.
[22] Ibid.

Sculptured House

GOLDEN, COLORADO

Charles Deaton (1965)

Above The futuristic form of the house offers a local landmark on the mountain top, visible from the valley below.

Opposite The clamshell surface of the building was made with poured concrete, which was then coated in a protective layer of synthetic rubber.

During the 1960s there was a wave of dynamic, sinuous buildings that spoke of the future, from the famous TWA terminal (1962) by Eero Saarinen (p. 120) at JFK Airport in New York, to Elrod House (1958; p. 210) in Palm Springs by John Lautner, as well as Charles Deaton's Sculptured House, perched high on top of Genesee Mountain, near Golden, Colorado. Visible for miles around, it soon became a local landmark and has remained so ever since.

Deaton first designed the house as a maquette, drawing inspiration from his love of the natural world. This sculpture took the form of a clamshell sitting on a plinth, cracked open to one side. Like his designs for expressive and eye-catching bank buildings, such as the Key Savings & Loan (1967) in Englewood, Colorado, Deaton's only residential design also turned its back on the strict, linear modernity of the International Style and embraced free-flowing curves and fluid lines.

'People aren't square, so why should they live in squares?' he wrote in *Art in America* magazine in the mid-1960s. 'I believe people look better and feel better among curves – they make people feel less confined. In other words, curved buildings provide a natural setting for curved people.'[23]

Having found some success with his commercial commissions, Deaton began to look for a site to turn his sculpted maquette into reality. An amateur pilot, he first spotted the Genesee Mountain site from the air, and managed to buy a fifteen-acre hilltop plot, with its epic views of the open landscape over the treetops below.

Beginning in 1963, he created the concrete pediment of the house, first using steel supporting rods tied to the bedrock. This pedestal supported the clamshell structure, which was made using a steel mesh cage that was then coated in concrete, pumped on site and finished with an outer layer of Hypalon, a kind of synthetic rubber, mixed with white pigment and ground walnut shells.

The shell of the house was completed in 1965, but construction costs were high, given the nature of the site and the unusual shape and engineering of the building. The interiors remained incomplete, with

Deaton and his family unable to move into the building but living nearby, on the same mountain, watching the house slowly evolve. It fell to Deacon's daughter, Charlee, and her husband, architect Nick Antonopoulos, to finish the house for a new owner.

'Around the time I was born, my father began sketching ideas for his dream house and it was very stop-start throughout my childhood,' Charlee Deaton says. 'As a family, we weren't in a position to save the house and it was painful to see it go. But we were able to produce the plans for John Huggins, who bought the house, and finish it so that it truly reflected – as my father put it – the "unencumbered song" that he wanted it to sing out.'[24]

Left Floor-to-ceiling glass in the living area provides a vast lens focused on the horizon; furniture includes pieces by Eero Saarinen and Arne Jacobsen.

Below The terrace offers an elevated viewing platform for appreciating the open views of the Colorado landscape.

Above Bedrooms and bathrooms offer edited glimpses of the outdoors, with the repeated use of sinuous curves throughout the interiors.

Opposite Furniture includes colourful designs by Pierre Paulin, Harry Bertoia and Arne Jacobsen, all in keeping with the 1960s aesthetic.

Antonopoulos, who worked in Deaton's architectural practice, created a discreet addition that tripled the available living space, while Charlee Deaton completed the interiors. The crowning glory is an interconnected sequence of living spaces that connect with both the open views and an elevated terrace via a curving wall of floor-to-ceiling glass. Sinuous lines become a repeated motif throughout, as seen in the curving form of the staircase and much of the integrated furniture and other features.

The Sculptured House is now on the US National Register of Historic Places. Yet it still continues, with its curvaceous

clamshell aesthetic, to speak of the future. Famously, Woody Allen used the house as a setting for the sci-fi comedy *Sleeper* (1973), set in 2173, two hundred years into the future. Both Deaton and the house received a mention in the film credits.

23 Kate Jacobs, 'Take Me Higher', in *Elle Decoration UK*, June 2004.
24 Ibid.

Sunnylands

RANCHO MIRAGE, CALIFORNIA

A. Quincy Jones (1966)

Above The interiors are complemented by a wide choice of garden rooms and halfway spaces between inside and out.

Opposite Landscaping softens the single-storey home, with an ornamental lake and integrated planting creating connections to the natural world.

Walter and Leonore Annenberg were dream clients. They were collectors of art and enlightened patrons of design, with the winning combination of ambition and generous budgets. With Sunnylands, their 200-acre estate in Rancho Mirage, California, the couple excelled themselves, creating a palatial exemplar of Desert Modernism by architect A. Quincy Jones and interior designer William Haines.

Walter Annenberg had made his fortune as a media magnate, building up the family's newspaper business and expanding into magazines, radio and television. From 1969 to 1974, he was a popular ambassador to the United Kingdom. After selling their media interests to Rupert Murdoch, the couple devoted much of their time to philanthropy.

For many years, they had enjoyed spending the winter months in Palm Springs, and began buying up land near the Tamarisk Country Club in Rancho Mirage, where Annenberg liked to play golf, and gradually built up a holding of nearly 1,000 acres of desert. Eventually, they decided that the time was right to build their own home and turned to Jones and Haines, who had worked on the interiors of the family's main residence in Wynnewood, Pennsylvania.

Both architect and designer already had long experience of working in the area – Jones designed the Palm Springs Tennis Club (1947), and Haines created interiors for the home of studio head Jack Warner – and had worked together on residential projects for Armand and Harriet Deutsch, good friends of the Annenbergs, and Sidney and Frances Brody. The Brodys were also supporters of modern architecture, and had commissioned Jones and Haines to design a house in Los Angeles, which was finished in 1949, complete with a mural by Henri Matisse.

The Annenbergs wanted a modern house, but they also wanted something that would be a true original. They shared a fondness for Mexico and suggested a Mayan theme for the building, expressed in the form of the vast pyramid roof floating over the main body of the structure. The house also needed to open itself up to the landscaped grounds, including an ornamental lake, swimming pool and private golf course.

Below Walls of lava blocks create distinctive textural contrasts with the marble floors and the sculptural concrete ceiling.

Right The atrium beneath the pyramid roof offers a dramatic circulation and reception space; it also doubled as an art gallery.

Jones created a design that fused the informal with the formal, and a sense of openness with more intimate spaces. The pink-tiled roof formed a vast canopy, accessed via an inviting porch. The entrance led into a generously scaled atrium, which also doubled as an open-plan living area with marble floors and a central skylight. Exposed steel beams and a sculptural ceiling create a gallery feel here, enhanced by the extraordinary art collection.

The main living spaces, including a spacious sitting room and dining room, circulate around the central atrium in a fluid and interconnected manner, while service spaces such as the kitchen and pantry are carefully hidden away. There are then three spokes,

Opposite The guest wing hosted two suites, plus this communal 'Game Room': a colourful lounge that was also used for showing movies.

Below The master bedroom, with interiors by William Haines; the painting over the bed is by Jacques Villon, dated 1952.

or wings, arranged around this communal heartland, with one holding the master suite and private ancillary spaces, as well as a staff wing and a guest wing.

There are constant connections with the landscape throughout, via banks of floor-to-ceiling glass that contrast with the solid, characterful walls made from lava blocks. The overhanging roof creates a veranda, complemented by a series of canopies and pergolas that further dissolve the distinctions between indoor and outdoor space. Overall, the scale of the house and its satellite buildings is almost palatial, yet the grounded

nature of the single-storey home prevents it from being overwhelming or competing with the setting and the mountain views.

Both family home and art gallery (many important pieces were later donated to the Metropolitan Museum of Art), Sunnylands was also a house for entertaining on a grand scale (Frank Sinatra celebrated his fourth marriage here) and served as a version of Camp David, hosting many political figures and world leaders. Architecturally, it marked a high point in the golden age of Californian mid-century Desert Modernism, focused upon Palm Springs and its environs.

Esherick Hedgerow House

SEA RANCH, CALIFORNIA

Joseph Esherick (1966)

The birth of Sea Ranch in the mid-1960s was accompanied by an almost Utopian set of ideals and a design manual that established its building codes. This new community on the rugged northern Californian coast sat within 4,000 acres, which once served a sheep farm, and both developers and architects wanted to preserve the beauty of the setting, applying a light touch that would dispense with such suburban features as street lighting and striped lawns. The aim was a kind of synergy between the settlement and its surroundings, with architecture that spliced vernacular references with modernist ideas and principles.

Early on, the developers Oceanic Properties began working with landscape architect Lawrence Halprin on ideas for the community and an environmentally friendly design philosophy. Halprin worked out a masterplan that would bundle the houses together in clusters, while preserving the openness of the landscape and the coastline itself. Sea views would be prioritized, utility services buried underground, and the original trees and planting preserved

as much as possible. Halprin and his wife Anna also built a house here for themselves, embracing the ethos of the community they helped to create, and even led creative workshops for its residents.

Oceanic Properties and Halprin began working with two architectural teams on the early designs for Sea Ranch. Architects Charles Moore, Donlyn Lyndon, William Turnbull and Richard Whitaker of MLTW, based in Berkeley, California, designed the first building, which resembled a collection of interconnected houses arranged around a central courtyard. Sited on a prominent position overlooking the coast, the timber-clad Condominium One included Moore's own home.

Like MLTW, Joseph Esherick was also influenced by vernacular ideas and the beauty of traditional barns and farmsteads. He was asked to design another cluster of individual demonstration houses, which would showcase the 'Sea Ranch style'. Known as Hedgerow Houses, these homes were built along the line of one of the windbreak hedges planted on the ranch in 1916.

Above The house references the vernacular in its use of shingles and timber, giving it an organic quality, yet the form is also distinctly modern.

Opposite Esherick's home adapts to the landscape's gentle shifts in level; planting is sensitive and naturalistic, with flagstone terraces to one side.

Esherick designed a series of four modest residences that shared similar principles and a common approach to materials, with timber frames, shingle cladding and simple mono-pitch roofs. The houses aimed to maximize connections to the coastal vista and the indoor–outdoor relationship, while using the hedgerows and the topography to create a degree of shelter from the sun and wind, which Esherick had studied with great care. As with the other Sea Ranch houses, there were no obvious boundaries or fences around them, enhancing the sense of connectivity with the landscape.

Just as Charles Moore took up residence at Condominium One, so Esherick decided to design a Hedgerow House for himself.

The living room features picture windows facing the ocean view and a wood-burning stove; much of the seating is built-in to maximize the available space within this compact home.

Below The bedrooms and bathroom up in the eaves also make use of every inch of space, with integrated storage space and shelving throughout.

It was the last and smallest of the series, at around 80 m² (875 sq ft), tucked into the gently sloping site, with a creek to the front, traversed by a bridge, and meadows to the rear. Esherick worked with the shifting levels, creating a large living room around a fireplace, integrated seating and windows facing the ocean. Two small bedrooms and a bathroom are at the far end of the house, with a third in a mezzanine level that floats above the kitchen/dining area. To the rear, he added a patio and a deck that feeds out from one of the bedrooms, while using the shape of the land to create some privacy for these outdoor rooms.

'The ideal kind of building is one you don't see,' Esherick once said, and his own house, which is full of discretion, lived up to the maxim. Yet the fluid nature of the living spaces was distinctly modern, as was the way the house maximized the views to the front with banks of windows, while gently turning its back to the meadow. As exemplars of a highly contextual, organic approach to architecture, Esherick's Hedgerow Houses are hugely influential, and Sea Ranch as a whole remains a vital reference point in terms of sustainable modern design.

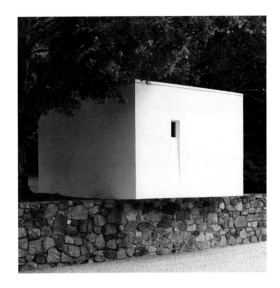

Stillman House II

LITCHFIELD, CONNECTICUT
Marcel Breuer (1966)

Above Walls of local stone help to tie the house to its setting; a pool sits to the rear, while a small guest house sits alongside the master building.

Opposite The single-storey building rests serenely in this semi-rural setting, surrounded by trees and looking across a gently dipping landscape.

During the postwar period, the former Bauhaus master Marcel Breuer designed and built around sixty houses. Many of these were in New England, and Connecticut, in particular, where Breuer developed his own special take on regional Modernism. Here, his residences tended to be either linear or 'bi-nuclear' homes, which offered a clear sense of separation between daytime living spaces, generally open plan, and bedroom retreats. These were houses that adopted crisp, clean lines and a vivid indoor–outdoor relationship, as one might expect from a dedicated modernist, but they were also contextual homes that responded to the region and the landscape, while making use of local materials such as stone, brick and timber.

Breuer's most loyal and devoted Connecticut client was Rufus Stillman, vice-president and later chairman of the Torin Corporation, which produced industrial fans and air-moving equipment. In 1948 Stillman and his wife Leslie visited Breuer's *House in the Museum Garden* exhibit at the Museum of Modern Art in New York, a full-scale but temporary showhouse created as an exemplar of modern living (it was later bought by the Rockefeller family as a guest lodge for their estate in Pocantino Hills). The Stillmans were so impressed by the project, also known as the MoMA Research House, that they sought out its architect and began a long and fruitful friendship.

Stillman actively promoted Breuer and his work, making him the architect of choice for the Torin Corporation. Breuer would eventually design a total of nine buildings for the company, both in Connecticut and further afield. Stillman also served on the board of trustees of the local school in Litchfield and played a crucial part in commissioning a number of educational and campus buildings during the 1950s, as well as recommending the architect to colleagues and friends.

On a more personal level, Stillman asked Breuer to design not just one, but three contemporary New England houses for himself and his family. 'We knew we had to build in our own time,' he said. 'If MoMA thought he was that good, then we shouldn't argue about it.'[25]

The use of brick floors, as well as stone for the fire hearths, also helps to root the house to the land, while adding textural depth and character to the interiors; large windows front and back frame key views of the grounds.

The first Stillman house was a variant of a 'long house', set upon a gentle hillside on the outskirts of Litchfield and completed in 1951. Fifteen years later, the Stillmans asked Breuer to design another house near Litchfield, which became known as Stillman House II. Here, again, the site is delightful, with the house sited upon the crest of a gentle slope within a clearing in the woods.

This time, Breuer adopted a bi-nuclear approach. The main body of the single-storey house was pushed gently into the hillside, with natural stone used for the retaining walls, helping to frame the building. A generous, open-plan living space sits at the heart of a U-shaped formation, opening out via a sliding bank of glass onto a semi-

Opposite In the lounge, at one end of the house, the fitted bookcases are original Breuer designs; the sofa and side tables are by Piero Lissoni.

Below The recent restoration has respected the original character of the building, while exploring the natural beauty of the materials.

sheltered terrace. The living area is set a few steps down from the terrace, enhancing the sense of height and volume, while the stonework carries into the house in the form of plinths for the side walls and the fireplace, complemented by brick floors. Bedrooms and bathrooms are positioned in the two wings to either side of this central space.

To one side of the main residence, Breuer designed a separate architectural echo that serves as a small guest pavilion, also adopting a linear outline and exterior walls of crisp, white stucco. This contrasts with the natural grey textures of the stone retaining walls, which carry out into the more sheltered rear garden, where Breuer created a swimming pool. Further down the garden, artist and sculptor Alexander Calder, who lived nearby,

created a mural upon a monolithic wall of concrete; the artist also painted murals at Stillman House I and, later, Stillman House III.

The house was completed in 1966, as was another of Breuer's most famous projects, the Whitney Museum of American Art in New York. Stillman House II has recently been restored and manages to still feel fresh, original and engaging, with a powerful relationship throughout between the building and its surroundings. The Stillmans asked Breuer to design a third house, completed in 1973, yet eventually found themselves going full circle and returning to Stillman House I in the 1990s.

25 Rachel Carley, *Litchfield: The Making of a New England Town* (Litchfield Historical Society, 2011).

Kappe Residence

PACIFIC PALISADES, CALIFORNIA

Ray Kappe (1967)

Above With its multiple shifts in level, the house and garden work their way around the steep hillside setting, with the planting a key part of the home.

Opposite Divisions between inside and out are eroded throughout, as seen in the elevated terrace, which projects outwards from the front of the house.

The design of Ray Kappe's family home in Pacific Palisades evolved from a specific dialogue with the land itself. The steep but verdant slope of the site, just to the north of Santa Monica and around 1.5 km (1 mile) from the ocean, was a key driver of the entire project. As such, it serves as an appropriate exemplar of Kappe's highly contextual approach to architecture, which splices elements of the 'organic' method promoted by Frank Lloyd Wright (p. 54) with the linear Modernism of Richard Neutra (p. 72) and many pioneering Californian modernists.

'My overriding attitude defines architecture as the achievement of equality between the user, the site and the surrounding environment, and the incorporation of environmental factors and the exploration of structure and materials,' Kappe has said.'[26]

The site that he and his wife, architectural historian Shelly Kappe, eventually chose was regarded by many as impossible to build upon. The slope is steep, but there is also an underground spring running through the property, which had to be taken into account. Given the restrictions created by the lack of load-bearing topography, Kappe decided to use six modest concrete towers, or cores, to anchor the house to the site. These cores are not only essential structural elements, but also hold many of the services, in particular the bathrooms, as well as a staircase leading down to a semi-basement storey, which itself holds a studio space.

Kappe used post-and-beam construction to create a light wooden framework for the rest of the house, supported by the concrete cores. In this way, the building became a kind of bridge made from laminated Douglas fir beams, which float over the slope while causing minimal interference with the land or spring. The 'bridge' is arranged across multiple but interconnected levels, with the main living spaces towards the centre, while the master suite is at the front of the site and the children's bedrooms at the rear. This fluid arrangement provides constant connectivity between the key spaces, yet still gives definition to areas such as the sitting room, dining room and kitchen.

'The greatest challenge was to get the towers into place, while disturbing the

Below The verdant greenery offers a natural backdrop to spaces such as the kitchen and adjoining dining area; the chairs are by Charles and Ray Eames.

Opposite The central portion of the house serves as a bridge between the concrete cores, becoming a series of half-levels within a multi-layered plan.

underground by the least amount,' Kappe noted in an interview in 2010. 'But what really pleases me most about the house now is the way that it relates to the sun during the day and the moon at night.'[27]

The cohesion of the interiors is further enhanced by the many bespoke and integrated pieces of furniture designed by the architect himself. These include fitted sofas, chairs, tables and many other items (largely made from warm redwood) that make best use of the available space, while also adding to the ordered yet organic feel of the house. At the same time, the combination of the contextual approach and extensive use of glazing allows for constant connections with the exteriors, enhanced

by elements such as the balcony to the front and adjoining terraces. Despite the challenges of the site, the natural surroundings still play a vital part in the atmosphere and ethos of the house, with its vivid indoor–outdoor relationship.

'My intention is always to blur the distinction between inside and out, but at the same time allow for separation where it is warranted,' Kappe added. 'My house has lots of glass and the view is of endless trees, so you feel like you're in a forest. The entire site is used as a garden, both underneath the house and on the roof.'[28]

[26] Hannah Booth, 'Beyond the Forest', *Elle Decoration UK*, March 2010.
[27] Interview with the author.
[28] Booth, 'Beyond the Forest'.

Compact bathrooms sit within the concrete cores, which are toplit by skylights, while the bedrooms feature vibrant splashes of colour along with integrated beds and storage designed by Kappe.

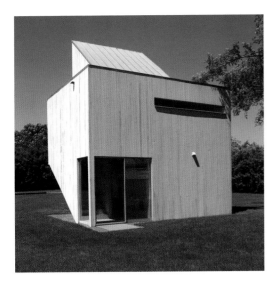

Gwathmey House & Studio

AMAGANSETT, NEW YORK

Charles Gwathmey (1965)

Above The house and studio form two complementary sculptural objects, sharing the same architectural language and materials.

Opposite The house is over three levels, with a studio on the ground floor and the living space at mid-level, accessible via the external stairway.

This house in the Hamptons, designed by Charles Gwathmey for his parents, can be seen as one of the great familial commissions. It was a generous act of faith, as he had only qualified as an architect a few years earlier, followed by a period spent in Europe visiting buildings by his architectural heroes, particularly Le Corbusier.

Upon his return, Gwathmey spent a short time working with Edward Larrabee Barnes, but gave up his job when his parents offered him, more or less, carte blanche. 'It was a very personal experience, and my parents did place a great deal of trust in me,' he explained. 'My mother said, "do what you would do for yourself". So I designed and built the house in a "naïve" spirit that was unencumbered and uncontaminated, while committed to a modern ethic.'[29]

His parents, Robert and Rosalie Gwathmey, had acquired an acre of land near Amagansett, not far from the sea, at a time when Long Island was still the preserve of potato farmers, but was being discovered by artists including Willem de Kooning and Jackson Pollock. They had a total of $50,000

to both buy the land, which cost around $15,000, and build the house. Having spoken with local contractors and realizing that it would be impossible to build the house he had in mind for such a limited budget, Gwathmey decided to act as the contractor himself, working alongside three craftsmen he brought over from Brooklyn.

There was another key compromise, as the young architect discovered that he would not be able to build with concrete, as he had hoped, and turned instead to a timber frame with cedar siding. Yet this decision did not affect the form of the house, which was influenced more by the inspiration of Le Corbusier, particularly the Chapel of Notre-Dame du Haut (1955) at Ronchamp, than by the vernacular influence of barns and silos, as later suggested by some commentators.

'I was very influenced by Le Corbusier at the time and wanted to make a volumetric building,' Gwathmey said. 'The modulation was all about ceiling height and form. Corbusier's plans were always very simple, but the spaces became very dynamic, spatial and complex. That was my motivation.'[30]

205

Opposite The main living area has a dramatic sense of height and volume; the two pairs of armchairs are by Le Corbusier and Marcel Breuer.

Below The master bedroom, which has the best of the views, sits on a mezzanine level above the dining area and kitchen below.

The brief called only for a living space, a bedroom/bathroom, and some space for the grandchildren. Gwathmey created a highly sculptural form, comprising a bunk room and small studio on the ground floor, and an open-plan, double-height living area that formed the piano nobile. Working around planning restrictions, he created a modest mezzanine at the top of the house, which offered views all the way to the ocean. The elegant, cohesive composition also contained a curvilinear external staircase and an integrated, semi-sheltered, elevated terrace alongside the main living space.

Around a year later, once they were settled in the house and enjoying the surroundings, Robert and Rosalie Gwathmey asked their

son to design and build a smaller, companion building alongside, holding a guest bedroom on the ground floor and a painting studio above. Gwathmey adopted the same language and materials, and the two structures dance together on the verdant plane of the lawn and simple garden.

The house launched Gwathmey's career, and is often regarded as his finest and most influential project. Following the death of his parents, he inherited the house and took up residence there himself, making only minor changes and updates within a subtle restoration programme. The house still has an engaging character and a timeless quality, as well as serving as a key marker in the evolution of postwar Modernism.

The sitting room within the piano nobile leads out to an elevated terrace alongside it, with banks of glass dissolving the line between inside and outside space, as well as drawing in the surrounding trees and greenery.

'It was very new at the time, with these two sculptural objects on a plane,' Gwathmey has said about the house. 'There is an irrefutability about its integrity and presence, its spatial variation, and its clarity and balance of solid and void. It catapulted my career, and confirmed that one must always take the risk. If not, one does not grow or discover as an artist.'[31]

[29] Interview with the author.
[30] Hannah Booth, 'Beyond the Forest'.
[31] Ibid.

Elrod House

PALM SPRINGS, CALIFORNIA

John Lautner (1968)

By 1960, when architect John Lautner designed the Chemosphere (1960), a modernist house in Hollywood, his projects tended to be defined by one dramatic, overarching idea. The concept for Chemosphere (also known as Malin House) was defined by an octagonal, geometric structure floating above a steeply sloping hillside on a single, concrete stem.

Two years later, Garcia House, also in the Hollywood Hills, was arranged beneath a vast roof sheltering the spaces beneath it. These big ideas were, increasingly, reliant on ambitious structural engineering and expressed in concrete.

By the late 1960s, Lautner's reputation as a sculptor of structure and form was secure, and so was that of Palm Springs as a city of modernist architectural experimentation, funded by an increasing number of Hollywood hedonists who used the desert retreat as an escape valve. Here, interior designer Arthur Elrod acquired a parcel of land up on Smoke Tree Mountain, with open views across the Coachella Valley floor and the city below.

Elrod had founded his practice in Palm Springs and was well connected with the Hollywood elite. Yet rather than design his own house, he turned to Lautner in the hope of creating something that was 'architecturally exceptional'. The architect did not disappoint him.

The key idea was the extraordinary circular living room, topped by a floating, propeller-like concrete roof, with semi-shaded skylights between the 'blades'. This pivotal, open space faced the landscape, framed by a band of floor-to-ceiling glass, which crossed the surface of a kidney-shaped pool that also inhabited part of the terrace beyond. This curving glass wall retracted to fully connect indoors and out, while the boundaries between them were blurred even further by rocks and boulders that pushed into the space. The floors were in dark slate, with a large fireplace to one side of the room.

'At night, with the house lights dimmed,' Lautner wrote, 'the black slate floor in the living room seems to disappear into the night and one finds oneself in space viewing the sparkling lights of Palm Springs.'[32]

Above The house is tucked into the rocky hillside, with the rounded prow of the guest wing sitting a little further down the slope.

Opposite The main living spaces sit under an extraordinary propeller-blade roof, with a wall of glass that retracts to form a seamless transition to the pool.

Below The staircase connecting the main living spaces to the guest quarters below has a highly sculptural quality of its own.

Right Rocks and boulders push into the circular living room and adjoining master suite; skylights complement the band of glazing facing the open view.

At 18 m (60 ft) across, this room has the grandeur of a theatre or place of worship. It played host to legendary parties, fashion shows and photoshoots, and starred in the James Bond film *Diamonds Are Forever* (1971), playing the part of Willard Whyte's mansion. Lautner positioned a kitchen to the rear of this multi-functional room, next to the entrance, while the master bedroom and bathroom sit to one side. Again, boulders infiltrate the interiors, creating a contrast between the natural and the artificial.

Opposite The kitchen sits to the rear
of the main living space and features a
collection of glass flowers by the artist
and sculptor Dale Chihuly.

Below The mountain rocks also form
a backdrop to the master bathroom (left),
while the guest bedrooms have a semi-
subterranean quality to them.

The house as a whole can be seen as
an evolution of the philosophy of organic
architecture championed by Lautner's former
mentor, Frank Lloyd Wright (p. 54), in which
buildings are designed as responses to the
site and surroundings. Here, on the mountain,
Lautner created high drama, but also pushed
the house into the hill while working around
the topography and its geology.

Later, Elrod asked Lautner to add a
separate guest wing, and this, too, was
integrated into the landscape. Positioned a
step down the slope and pushing out from it
like the bow of a ship, this part of the house
also explores rounded forms but, at times,
takes on a semi-subterranean character.
Certainly, the hierarchy of the building
remains clear, with the dominance of the
propeller room unchallenged. Later projects
continued to focus on the drama of the
roofscape and fluid forms, as Lautner took
architectural showmanship to new heights,
helping, along with Eero Saarinen (p. 120),
to inspire the fresh dynamism of a number
of 21st-century architects.

32 Frank Escher, ed., *John Lautner: Architect* (London:
Artemis, 1994).

Round House

WILTON, CONNECTICUT
Richard Foster (1968)

The idea of circular living was explored by a number of architects during the mid-century period – from Arne Jacobsen in Denmark to Roy Ground in Australia and Wolfgang Ewerth in Morocco. Yet none of these buildings was quite as dynamic as Richard Foster's Round House, which turns slowly on a central axis to follow the sun and shift perspective on the surrounding landscape.

The house makes the most of its setting in every way. Built on the bluff of a hill, looking across woodland and down towards the local reservoir, the entire house revolves 360° to frame different aspects of this bucolic setting on the green edges of Wilton, Connecticut. Completed in 1968, Foster's house – shared with his wife and their three sons – was his most original residential project, and captured international attention almost as soon as it was completed.

Approached along a narrow, sloping driveway, the house reveals itself as a sculptural, shingle-coated form, standing out against the green backdrop of the pines. It floats upon a slender central stem, which holds the spiral staircase, and around which the entire house slowly pivots on demand. The undercroft serves as a large circular veranda, paved with stone cobbles, which becomes an extraordinary outdoor room, sheltered, yet open to the countryside.

'The site is a natural amphitheatre and the earlier plans didn't take full advantage of it,' said Foster about the project in the *New York Times* on 3 September 1968. 'When the idea came to me, the only problem was finding the right parts. As far as I know, this hasn't been done before in this country.'

The interiors are all on one level – an elevated piano nobile, arranged radially in segments, looking out towards windows surrounding the house and the balcony. The original plan included a large living room, with partitions that enclosed a separate dining room, a galley-style kitchen and three bedrooms, plus a den; compact bathrooms of the kind one might find in a ship's cabin were arranged around an inner ring, bordering a landing that wrapped around the stair core. This core is topped by a skylight that introduces a rich burst of additional sunlight into the heart of the house.

Above he living spaces are bordered by a circular balcony, which resembles a ship's deck, a feeling enhanced by the gradual movement of the building.

Opposite Seen from afar, the hillside position and context of the house becomes clear; the land dips away to the right and towards the reservoir.

Above The circular hallway is the pivot point around which the house revolves; the living area and bedrooms all radiate from this space.

Opposite A recent restoration has included updates to the swimming pool and former garage and store, which now serves as a spa and guest lodge.

With such a sense of openness, the house becomes a kind of futuristic belvedere, but one in which there are multiple choices about how to position it according to the view. The building takes forty-eight minutes to fully rotate on a ball-bearing mechanism, inspired by moving radar antennae, and is controlled by a set of buttons marked 'for' (forward), 'rev' (reverse) and 'stop', while running on power from a small motor.

The design required a great deal of ingenuity, not only in terms of the turning mechanism, but also the way in which services and drainage manage to continue working around the turning circle. The electrical circuit is maintained by a ring

system, while water is collected in a circular tray and neatly drained away via a single conduit. The concealed attic holds many of the services of the house within a large 'engine room', with the water drawn from an on-site spring.

The house has recently been renovated by new owners, who asked Mack Scogin Merrill Elam Architects to work on the project. The original cedar shingles, cobbled veranda and many other elements were restored, and services updated. The original swimming pool was replaced with a new saltwater pool, and the former garage to one side was replaced with a guest room and spa space tucked into the hillside and topped with a deck.

Architects Mack Scogin Merrill Elam updated the interiors, creating a balance between fluid, interconnected living spaces and more private retreats, such as the master bedroom.

For Foster, the building was a pilot for the principle of rotating houses, but he did not complete any similar projects, and other commissions took him towards some very different typographies. An advertisement from *Time* magazine in 1976 for 'Old Grand-Dad' bourbon featured a picture of the house accompanied by the words: 'Pine forests, rolling hills, lakes and a house that rotates to take it all in … What more could you ask for?'

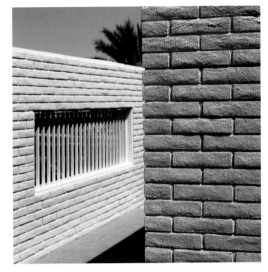

Palevsky House

PALM SPRINGS, CALIFORNIA
Craig Ellwood (1970)

Although Max Palevsky made his fortune in computer technology, he also had a passion for art and architecture. Born in Chicago, he studied science, mathematics and philosophy, before becoming a tech pioneer in the early 1950s, working with Packard Bell and others. In 1961 Palevsky founded Scientific Data Systems, and nine years later the company was sold to Xerox, making close to $1 billion.

This fortune enabled Palevsky to pursue his love of art as a collector and patron, becoming a key supporter of the Museum of Contemporary Art in Los Angeles and helping to bankroll a number of Hollywood films. He was also fascinated by architecture, and eventually became one of Craig Ellwood's most important and loyal clients.

By 1966, when Ellwood completed a production plant for Scientific Data Systems in El Segundo, California, the two men were good friends, and when Palevsky bought a prime parcel of land on the edge of Palm Springs, it was a natural decision to ask Ellwood to design a new retreat here, not far from Richard Neutra's Kaufmann Desert House (p. 72).

Privacy was a key concern. Previously, Palevsky had owned a weekend and winter apartment in Los Angeles, but wanted something with an escapist quality, where he could be at home with the desert landscape. Both architect and client were drawn to the idea of a walled compound, and even visited Morocco and Tunisia to see the walled farmsteads common to the region.

Along with his colleague Alvaro Vallejo, Ellwood designed a rectangular, walled compound, 200 m (656 ft) long and 90 m (295 ft) wide, with an arrangement of pavilions, terraces and courtyards. To the rear of the site, he positioned the entry sequence, a garage and a guest pavilion, separated from Palevsky's own residence by a substantial courtyard. The main pavilion is also single storey and steel-framed, designed to connect with the pool terrace beyond via a wall of glass, protected by a sun canopy.

One's gaze is carried over the swimming pool and terrace towards the open desert, with the brick walls of the compound interrupted here and replaced with a low, translucent screen that allows the vista to

Above Brick walls surround much of the compound, protecting the master residence, the guest house, the courtyards and terraces.

Opposite The main residence and pool terrace are focused on a view framed between the walls, with the gap protected by a translucent screen.

Opposite A large painting by Roy Lichtenstein is a colourful backdrop to the dining area, which forms part of an open-plan living space.

Below Artworks by Donald Judd punctuate the walls either side of the fireplace, which anchors the seating area in the main residence.

be revealed. The side walls of the compound help to channel and enhance the views, while providing the sense of enclosure, protection and privacy that Palevsky wanted. The arrangement of the separate pavilions also lend a welcome degree of separation between host and visitors.

Palevsky House was a key project for Ellwood, one in which he was able to move away from a single, linear structure and develop a more complex design comprising multiple elements. Yet the focus on light, ethereal buildings remains, as does the relationship between inside and outside space – a hallmark of Ellwood's work – facilitated by the use of steel frames and curtain walls. The use of the compound helps to reduce the house's visual impact, and serves as a key marker in the evolution of the modern courtyard home, in which these outdoor rooms introduce light and air, while enhancing the impression of open space.

Palevsky was delighted with the house and introduced works of art by Roy Lichtenstein, Andy Warhol and others, as well as a large sculpture by Alexander Calder. For Ellwood, this was one of his last and most accomplished Californian houses, before he retired and moved to Italy. He was helped in this by Palevsky's gift of some stocks and shares in the Integrated Electronics Corporation, better known as Intel.

Frey House II

PALM SPRINGS, CALIFORNIA

Albert Frey (1964)

Above The house is tucked into the rugged topography of the mountain, adapting itself to the terrain, rather than imposing itself upon it.

Opposite Banks of floor-to-ceiling glass connect the interiors to the dramatic landscape, while the tin roof protects the house from the sun.

Like many architects, Albert Frey saw his own living spaces as opportunities for experimentation, where he was free to explore new ideas without fielding the usual requests and demands of a client. After settling in Palm Springs in the 1930s, the Swiss-born émigré used the design and build of his own houses as important markers within the evolution of his unique version of Desert Modernism.

Frey's first house in Palm Springs, completed in 1940, was one of the earliest truly modern homes in the Coachella Valley. It was modest, with a combined living area and bedroom, and a compact bathroom and kitchenette, yet forged a vibrant indoor–outdoor relationship, with the interiors carrying outwards to the terraces and views of the San Jacinto mountains. Projecting 'wing walls' helped to extend the building into the surrounding desertscape, while carrying the eye along with them. Later, Frey added a pool and a small guest house.

Frey House I was widely published, attracting new clients, and many of the ideas it contained were continued through into new projects, including Raymond Loewy House (1947), which took indoor–outdoor living to a new level. Some years later, Frey remodelled Frey House I, adding a distinctive upper level comprising an aluminium-clad circular tower with a series of periscope windows. But in the early 1960s, he sold it, and it was eventually demolished.

The site and setting for the next house were not so far away, but radically different in character. The first house was located on the flatlands of the valley floor, but for the second, Frey was tempted into the mountains themselves. He chose an extraordinary spot, at an elevation of around 67 m (220 ft), commanding a view of Palm Springs below. As the site was believed to be impossible to build on, he was able to buy the land cheaply and found himself in splendid isolation.

'I studied the position of the sun for a whole year,' Frey explained. 'My partner and I put up a ten-foot pole [3 m], and we measured the shadow from it and made a diagram, so we knew where the sun was at any time of the year. The plan was designed so that, for instance, the glass walls are

227

Below The house is all about connectivity, including the idea of framing the open vistas of the valley below.

Opposite Vast boulders push their way into the open-plan living and sleeping area, which features integrated seating and storage designed by Frey.

not exposed to the sun in the heat of the summer. That's what determined these overhangs. In winter, when the sun is much lower, it comes in and helps heat the house.'[33]

Like the original home, this new house was also modest in scale, at less than 93 m² (1,000 sq ft). Frey pushed the building into the mountainside, so that the rocks thrust their way into it, seen most dramatically in the combined living, dining and sleeping space, where it feels as though an avalanche has carried a vast boulder through one side of the house. The steel framework allows for walls of glass, framing the dramatic views, while the overhang of the metal roof helps protect the building from the sun and natural ventilation keeps it cool.

Frey designed the built-in furniture in the universal space, which forms two-thirds of the floorplan. Beyond are a small bathroom and compact kitchen. Glass walls slide open to allow an immediate connection with the vista, along with a terrace and a swimming pool, which feels both delightful and incongruous in this mountain setting.

With this project, Frey sought a kind of synergy with the land itself. This is a house of great invention and discretion, tucked into the rocks, where the architect was able to enjoy an intimate relationship with the natural world. Upon his death, he bequeathed the house to the Palm Springs Art Museum.

33 Jennifer Golub, *Albert Frey: Houses 1 & 2* (New York: Princeton Architectural Press, 1999).

Douglas House

HARBOR SPRINGS, MICHIGAN

Richard Meier (1973)

Even as the scale and complexity of his projects increased over time, residential commissions retained a particular hold on architect Richard Meier. His houses can be seen, as he himself has suggested, as important staging posts within the evolution of a highly individual design philosophy, which placed great emphasis on the positive manipulation of light and volume within crisp, precise geometrical forms.

Meier carried these ideas with him as he progressed from the relatively modest domestic scale to the galleries and museums with which he is most associated. 'Projects designed to accommodate and give expression to the private lives of others have proven to be a way forward in the continued development of my work,' he wrote. '[They allow] one to formulate ideas and develop a set of principles that, one hopes, will inform future work for a long time to come.'[34]

Of Meier's early houses, from the 1960s and '70s, the most dramatic and daring is Douglas House, near Harbor Springs, situated towards the northern tip of Lake Michigan. It is the setting, perched upon the steep bank, as much as the building itself, which creates this sense of drama. Surrounded by trees, it looks down onto a beach and out across the open waters of the lake, which has the epic quality of an inland sea. The ordered composition of this linear house stands out vividly against the green backdrop of the trees; from within, it frames not only vistas of the lake, but also vivid glimpses of the treetops.

'So steep is the slope to the water that the house appears to have been dropped into the site, a machine-crafted object that has landed in a natural world,' Meier wrote. 'The dramatic dialogue between the whiteness of the house and the primary blues and greens of the water, trees and sky allows the house not only to assert its own presence, but also to enhance, by contrast, the beauty of its natural environment.'[35]

Given the combination of the steep, sloping topography and its orientation towards the lake view, the house is accessed via a bridge-style walkway from the rear and at the uppermost of four levels, which contain within them a number of volumetric

Above Accessed via a bridge that leads into the uppermost level of the house, the building steps down the slope of the hillside by degrees.

Opposite Much of the house's drama stems from the contrast between the precision of the architecture and the extraordinary natural setting.

The four levels of the house embrace many volumetric and spatial shifts, including a central atrium that erodes the traditional idea of a tiered, linear formation, while creating highly dynamic interiors.

shifts, including a triple-height atrium. The main sitting room, at mid-level, faces sheets of glass overlooking the water, which also surround a boxed fireplace. These open, soaring spaces connect with a series of integrated decks that serve as viewing platforms, with an external stair providing an alternative to the interior route.

The house certainly makes the most of its surroundings, with its balconies and terraces reminiscent of the work of Le Corbusier and Eileen Gray, whose E-1027 (1929) on the French Mediterranean coast feels like a spiritual forerunner. Bedrooms and service spaces are pushed to the rear of the plan, allowing the key living areas facing the lake to enjoy the special sense of openness.

Douglas House forms one of a number of Meier's early, formative residences, which explored many common themes. Smith House (1967) in Darien, Connecticut, in particular feels like a cousin to the Lake Michigan project, perhaps because of its waterfront setting overlooking Long Island Sound.

But one also sees similar experiments with light, geometry and contrasts between openness and enclosure at Hoffman House (1967) and Saltzman House (1969), both on Long Island. Together, these residences form a fascinating, accomplished and rewarding early phase of Meier's architectural career.

34 Richard Meier, *Richard Meier: Houses & Apartments* (New York: Rizzoli, 2007).
35 Meier, *Richard Meier: Architect* (Oxford: Oxford University Press, 1976).

A series of decks, linked by an external stairway, help to erode the boundaries between inside and out, while offering tempting platforms for enjoying the open views of the lake and the natural beauty of the surroundings.

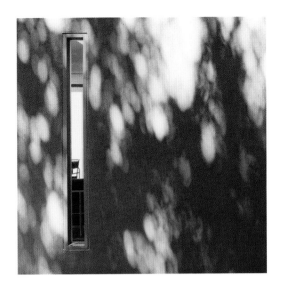  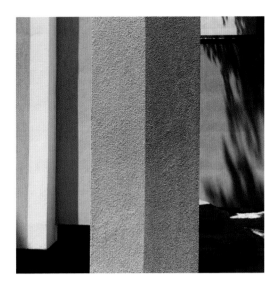

House VI

CORNWALL, CONNECTICUT

Peter Eisenman (1975)

Above House VI resembles a traditional house that has been pulled apart and reassembled like a disjointed three-dimensional puzzle.

Opposite A cabin in the woods like no other, the house offers a very different experiential quality within, yet still connecting with nature without.

It is not always easy living in a house of ideas. This was certainly the experience of art historian Suzanne Frank and her husband Dick, a photographer, at House VI in rural Connecticut. It is a house that is, as writer and art critic Kenneth Frampton described it, a 'canonical work'. Yet it is also the couple's family home, and the process of designing it strained the relationship between clients and architect to something close to breaking point.

Suzanne Frank was, and still is, a great admirer of Peter Eisenman. She had noted and respected the architect's work for many years, before asking if he would be willing to design a modest, low-budget house on a six-acre parcel of land that she and her husband had acquired in northwestern Connecticut. The land came with a small schoolhouse, which the couple eventually converted into a guest lodge, and a dilapidated Victorian structure they decided to demolish, recycling the foundations for their new home.

The commission began in a positive fashion, with Eisenman accepting his clients' small budget, and the Franks – who were content to grant him 'poetic licence' – happy to believe their new weekend and holiday house would be the latest in a sequence of innovative residences that formed the early phase of Eisenman's career. But over time, the 'theoretically aggressive' plans for the house, as writer William Gass described them, challenged so many conventions within a process of architectural deconstruction that House VI became more of a laboratory than a home.

The outward form and composition of the house were, in a sense, the easy part. Rather like Robert Venturi's Vanna Venturi House (p. 168) in Philadelphia, Eisenman twisted and subverted expectation to create an avant-garde variant on the American house. House VI could be described as a subversive cabin in the woods, a two-storey narrative of irregular slabs and apertures woven into a new form.

'I was looking for ways of conceptualizing space that will place the subject in a displaced relationship, because they will have no iconographic references to traditional forms of organization,' Eisenman explained.

237

Slots, lines, cuts and incisions challenge conventional notions of 'rooms' and living spaces, even within a house that is modestly scaled.

'That is what I have always been trying to do – to displace the subject – to oblige the subject to reconceptualize architecture.'[36]

Inside, this process of displacement continued without compromise. The Franks found that many of their requests, such as a fireplace, ended up on the cutting-room floor and that key spaces, like the kitchen, were close to impractical. Some architectural gestures, including the ghost staircase floating over the dining area, were delightful, but others, such as the introduction of a slot in the floor of the bedroom, which originally required the couple to sleep in two separate single beds, spoke of authorial arrogance.

Despite such challenges, Suzanne Frank was initially captivated by her first impressions of the house. 'In contrast to the

solidity of the exterior, the inside felt open,' she wrote in her book about the house. 'Light filtered in, and for a moment life seemed a careless spiritual existence. It was the quiet and dynamic spirituality I sensed that sustained my fondness for the house over the course of many years when we made our weekend jaunts to it.'[37]

Yet over time, frustrations began to creep in and 'differences' emerged between architect and clients over this house of ideas. There were the practical, day-to-day challenges of living in it, and it was poorly built and began to take in water after just a few years. These problems caused tensions to rise and, by 1987, the house was in such poor condition that the Franks had to virtually rebuild it. Fortunately, even after

Opposite A ghost staircase in vivid red is one of the most surprising elements in the house, offering an echo of the functional stairway below.

Below The upper level includes one bedroom, plus a sleeping alcove and bathroom, as well as moments for simply enjoying the landscape.

such a fraught journey, with many worries over financing repairs to the house, architect and clients were reconciled. Eisenman declared himself happy with the renovations and, at last, the Franks were able to take pleasure in their home.

'I have been told that the house represents what is best in Peter Eisenman's oeuvre,' Suzanne Frank wrote. 'I, too, think that the house is special – special because it holds memories of my family's lives, and because its formal structure is so right to the eye and its internal space accommodates our daily existence well. Not that the slot in the bedroom floor and the constant need for

a stepladder in the kitchen are not sources of annoyance and signs of Eisenman's arrogance. They certainly are. Not that I do not have unhappy times in it. Even the most ideal surroundings sometimes hold the seeds of discontent. But generally I could not ask for a lovelier experience.'[38]

[36] Philip Jodidio, *Contemporary American Architects*, vol. 2 (Cologne: Taschen, 1996).
[37] Suzanne Frank, *Peter Eisenman's House VI* (New York: Whitney Library of Design, 1994).
[38] Ibid.

Gerald Ford Estate

RANCHO MIRAGE, CALIFORNIA
Welton Becket & Associates (1978)

For Gerald and Betty Ford, their new home in the Coachella Valley represented a very welcome escape. After Gerald Ford's defeat to Jimmy Carter in the 1976 presidential election, the couple withdrew to the resort of Rancho Mirage, a few miles from Palm Springs, where they asked Welton Becket & Associates to design a six-bedroom, single-storey home, next door to Ginger Rogers and overlooking the Thunderbird Country Club golf course, a blaze of green in the desert.

It proved the perfect setting to recover from a gruelling re-election campaign, and offered Betty Ford a quiet retreat away from the glare of publicity, where she was able to confront addictions to alcohol and prescribed painkillers. Following her recovery, she founded the Betty Ford Center in 1982, and went on to produce two books on the subject of dependency. The house provided a stable base for the couple, where they both lived until the end of their lives.

Welton Becket, who died in 1969, was one of the mid-century Californian master architects. His projects included the distinctive circular Capitol Records Building

(1956) in Los Angeles and the Beverly Hilton Hotel (1953), as well as the Santa Monica Civic Auditorium (1958). He also designed houses for Hollywood celebrities and tract houses in Panorama City.

The Fords' house sits on a parcel of land that was once part of the neighbouring Firestone estate, which features a house designed by Becket's contemporary, William Pereira (p. 132). Like Pereira's design, it is single storey, and seeks to finely balance a welcome degree of privacy with a sense of openness to the grounds of the country club and the mountain views beyond.

The private driveway sweeps round to meet an elegant entry sequence, bordered by integrated planters, populated by trees and shrubs that help soften the rendered, horizontal bands protecting the front of the house. The entrance hallway is illuminated by high clerestory windows, which spill sunlight onto the brickwork floors. The current owners have introduced a large portrait of Betty Ford, which once hung in the White House and is now one of the first points of reference upon stepping inside.

Above The house offers an open relationship with the neighbouring golf course, while integrated planters help to soften the architecture.

Opposite The terraces around the pool offer a more secluded and private fresh-air setting, while connecting directly with key living spaces inside.

Opposite In the dining room, the table, chairs, rug and mural, which is by Garth Benton, are all original to the house.

Below The sitting room features armchairs and a rug by Darren Brown, and a sofa that is original to the house; the coffee table is by Steve Chase.

Towards the rear, the building opens up to the courtyard, which holds the swimming pool. Banks of floor-to-ceiling sliding-glass windows blur the division between inside and outside space, while drawing light deep into the living areas and bedrooms. Landscaping and planting around the courtyard preserves privacy, without blocking the vista.

The current owners, who acquired the house after Betty Ford died in 2011, asked architectural firm Marmol Radziner to update the property, the same practice that restored Richard Neutra's Kaufmann Desert House (p. 72) in Palm Springs. Systems were upgraded throughout, with a solar array fitted to the roof, providing electricity and hot water. Landscape designer Marcello Villano refreshed the planting and terraces, and interior designer Darren Brown was able to preserve or re-purpose a number of items of furniture that belonged to the Fords.

'We got quite a few pieces with the purchase of the house,' the owners explain. 'We would take a sofa or a chair and get it recovered, then we would save the fabric from the drapes and the chairs and have them made into bedspreads, so nothing was wasted.'

Below The luxurious master bathroom offers a large tub bordered with character stonework, matching the walls and vanity counter.

Opposite In this guest bedroom, the headboard and bedside tables are by Darren Brown and the artwork is by Wally Beshty.

Joe & Etsuko Price Residence

CORONA DEL MAR, CALIFORNIA

Bart Prince (1989)

Above Beautifully detailed, the house offers texture, colour and pattern, as well as sculptural forms, as seen in the stained glass and shingles.

Opposite The house sits on the brow of a hill, with banks of glass focused on the gardens like lenses sitting within the complex body of the building.

Although educated as an engineer, Joe Price's twin passions were always art and architecture. As a student at the University of Oklahoma, Price met Bruce Goff (p. 78), who was head of the architecture department at the time. Eventually, he asked Goff to build a house for him in Bartlesville, Oklahoma. The architect also introduced him to Frank Lloyd Wright (p. 54), who designed – at Price's suggestion – a skyscraper in the same city for his father's oil company, known as Price Tower (1956).

Having spent a number of years working in Japan on the design for the Imperial Hotel in Tokyo, it was Wright who also sparked Price's enduring passion for Japanese art and culture. In the early 1960s, Price turned his back on engineering and travelled in Asia, where he met his future wife, Etsuko. Together, the couple created an extraordinary collection of Japanese art and helped to fund the development of the Pavilion for Japanese Art at the Los Angeles County Museum, designed – of course – by Goff and his tutorial student-turned-colleague, Bart Prince.

Years later, when the Prices decided to commission a new house in California, they came back to see Prince, with whom they had struck up a friendship. They had acquired a parcel of land at Corona del Mar, near Newport Beach, south of Los Angeles. Naturally, for an architect and clients with a love of an organic and contextual approach to architecture, the house developed as a unique response to the site, as well as to the particular needs of the family.

'The Price residence offered a great opportunity to create something beautiful for wonderful people who were and are my friends, and on a site that is certainly among nature's best,' says Prince. 'Any true work of architecture should grow as an organism, which is experienced and understood from any direction, whether from within or without as a unified entity.'[39]

With its undulating, sinuous roof clad in timber shingles, the two-storey house seems to emerge from the land itself, partially enveloping an entry courtyard, complete with a Japanese-style gravel garden and planting. A series of overlapping pods hold the two

Above The shingle-coated roof has the sculpted, organic feel of an animal's back, complemented by the greenery of the garden setting.

Opposite The entrance courtyard offers a borderland between inside and out, setting a tempting tone for the journey into and around the house.

principal levels, with the main living spaces on the lowermost of these, while the upper level hosts the study, bedrooms and dens. Given the design of the courtyard, along with decks and elevated terraces facing the views, the boundaries between inside and out are constantly blurred.

'Sometimes you can't tell which is which,' Prince explains. 'My ideas grow from an "inside-out" response. They were not forced in order to achieve some preconception of form, but became that shape as a result of the spaces within and without. The form of this building results from the materials and construction methods that made it.'[40]

The biomorphic character of the exterior carries into the interiors, which feature many bespoke and integrated pieces of furniture,

largely made from wood. The structural glulam beams that support the house are made from fir, while the floors are in teak and the cabinets are in rosewood. Bespoke stained-glass windows, also designed by Prince, add splashes of colour and pattern.

This unique house is clearly organic in its architectural approach, yet also finely crafted. There are echoes of Japan, but the building is also reminiscent of the handcrafted and all-encompassing interiors of master woodworkers such as Wharton Esherick (p. 30) and George Nakashima (p. 144). At the same time, it feels like something that has arrived from another world and possesses a striking degree of cinematic futurism.

[39] Interview with the author.
[40] Ibid.

The main living spaces draw warmth and character from the crafted natural materials, including the timber floors and exposed glulam beams.

Greenberg House

LOS ANGELES, CALIFORNIA
Ricardo Legorreta (1991)

One of Ricardo Legorreta's earliest and most influential projects was the Camino Real hotel in Mexico City. Completed in 1968, it was a statement of intent, full of colour and texture, with a particular sense of balance between its courtyards, pools and outdoor rooms. The hotel was both modern and truly Mexican, drawing inspiration from the work of Legorreta's mentor Luis Barragán. The influence of Louis Kahn (p. 156) is also evident, giving the building its distinctive scale and monumentality.

'I met Barragán late in life and we developed a very good friendship, based on conversations about life, rather than design,' Legorreta says. 'We had very similar sources of inspiration – the old ranches, towns and villages of Mexico, as well as its artists and painters, especially in the use of colour. Here, we have the combination of two cultures – Hispanic and Indian – which has led to the development of a special sense of scale.'[41]

Taking this design philosophy with him, Legorreta began to work beyond Mexico. There were museums, a cathedral, factories and libraries – buildings of scale – yet even within many of his smaller residential projects, there is a clear predisposition towards an architecture of mass and monumentality. This is seen in his design for Greenberg House, which followed an earlier commission, also in Los Angeles, for the actor Ricardo Montalbán.

Designed for Arthur N. Greenberg and his family, the house fuses two architectural approaches across two elevations. From the front, it appears relatively closed – a mass of irregular linear blocks with high, sandy-coloured walls forming a protective courtyard entrance, flanked by a garage and a bedroom wing. Vertical incisions pierce the closed walls, creating a rhythmic quality to a building that appears enigmatic and mysterious, rather like a pueblo or a fortress.

'We love surprises, and we love mystery,' Legorreta adds. 'We say that we are very simple, but really we are extremely complicated. We are also very influenced by pre-Hispanic architecture in the sense of an almost Spartan aesthetic. Pre-Columbian architecture has the idea of mass and stone, painted with colours.'[42]

Above Strong lines, surfaces of colour and disciplined detailing create a house of great character, infused with a sense of monumentality.

Opposite The relatively closed planes of the façade and entrance courtyard create an enigmatic journey of discovery through the house.

To the rear, the house opens up to the garden, with a strong interplay between the building and the adjoining terraces, as they step down gradually towards the swimming pool. The form of the house is revealed more clearly here, with two towers holding a studio and master suite/library. An external staircase reaches down to the garden, enhancing the sense of a ziggurat.

'There is a dynamic between inside and out that we constantly enjoy,' Greenberg notes. 'There is an incredible quality of light, wonderful colours, human-scale rooms, amazing views and a very warm atmosphere. The beautiful landscaping makes us feel as though we are walking through a garden, even when we are indoors.'[43]

The positioning of the generous living spaces at the centre of the house, between the two towers, allows this sense of connection between the key rooms and the exteriors to be maximized to the full. A long sequence of glass frames the landscape, and accentuates the juxtaposition between the largely closed front elevation and the more open environment beyond. From the entrance to the garden, a glorious *promenade architecturale* solves the mystery of the house by degrees, while offering series of glorious surprises along the way.

[41] Interview with the author.
[42] Ibid.
[43] Ibid.

The house unfolds dramatically to the rear gardens, where a series of terraces and semi-shaded outdoor rooms lead down towards the swimming pool and lawn.

T-House

WILTON, NEW YORK
Simon Ungers (1992)

Set among the trees, in the woods near Saratoga Springs, Simon Ungers's T-House has the look of an extraordinary piece of land art. The building, coated in sheets of rusting Corten steel, has an abstract, earthy quality, and stands out against the verdant backdrop of the trees and sky.

The main, single-storey portion of the house could be described as a 'landscraper', tucked into the sloping topography of the site, but it is topped by a tower that forms a floating T-bar, hovering above the rest of the building and sitting among the treetops. In such a natural, even bucolic, setting, the presence of this enigmatic form is surprising and fascinating.

The house is the best-known work by Ungers, a German–American architect who worked at the complex interface between art and architecture. His buildings are, for the most part, tectonic sculptures, defined by striking compositions, abstraction and minimalism. They challenge conventional notions of house and home, adding fresh layers of meaning and modernity that invigorate the imagination.

The house was commissioned by writer and academic Lawrence Marcelle and his wife, Diane, who wanted both a weekend retreat and, importantly, a space to house a collection of over 10,000 books. Ungers designed the house in collaboration with Tom Kinslow as a one-off partnership.

'I became good friends with Tom and Simon, and spent a good deal of time talking with and listening to them,' Lawrence Marcelle says. 'While we had many discussions about aesthetics and architecture, I had no role in the design, which went through many changes, dealing mainly with proportions and ratios. But the final design was extremely close to the original. In many ways, the changes that were ultimately rejected constituted a proof of the soundness of the original design.'[44]

The Marcelles wanted a place to live and work, with a sense of space and distinction between these two realms, but also desired the house to be unusual and to provide a 'kind of protection and distance from the outside world'. Ungers and Kinslow settled on Corten steel for the house's exterior shell.

Above The abstract form and strong materiality of the building place it at the intersection of architecture and land art.

Opposite The woodland setting helps to ensure that the artificial geometry of the building and its rusting Corten coat stand out all the more vividly.

The plates of rust red Corten steel are, in one respect, semi-industrial in character, yet the colour and texture also have an earthy, almost organic quality, making the material enigmatic.

The material has been used for commercial buildings since the 1960s, but this was a relatively early residential application for use; in recent years, it has become more widely used for houses and cabins by, among others, Tom Kundig (p. 302). The Corten is designed to rust, forming a protective outer layer that appears industrial, mineral and semi-organic, enriched by its patina, texture and colour palette, with echoes of the earth and tree bark. It is also reminiscent of the monumental work of sculptors such as Richard Serra.

Inside, Ungers and Kinslow respected the wish for a sense of separation between daily living and the library. The living spaces have a crafted quality, with timber for the floors and ceilings, as well as the integrated furniture and joinery. The tower library, accessed via a modest staircase, is arranged over two levels, with a study and seating area below and the books on a mezzanine above, set within an ordered sequence of steel shelves; slim windows frame views of the trees. This is Lawrence Marcelle's favourite space, and the T-House certainly met his request for something truly unique.

'In the wider sense of its importance to architecture, I would say that it shows the strength and power of the modern in classical forms and pleasing ratios,' he says. 'It also shows that what we mean by a "house" is not something fixed and settled, but is open for contestation. Since the word "home" runs very deep in our language, this is not a trivial reminder.'[45]

[44] Interview with the author.
[45] Ibid.

The double-layered library and study sit within the T-bar of the house and feature custom-designed racks of shelving, which holds around 10,000 books.

Turtle Creek House

DALLAS, TEXAS

Antoine Predock (1993)

Turtle Creek House has two distinct personalities. Towards the street, the façade is largely closed and enigmatic, featuring a monumental stone ziggurat, interspersed with native wildflowers that soften the outline of the building. The impression is of a pre-Hispanic temple, worn by time and nature, punctured by a gateway that forms the main entrance. This façade connects closely with Antoine Predock's fascination with geology and tectonics, with the context of New Mexico and the southern states, and with Modernism. From this elevation, the building hardly looks like a house at all.

As it faces the private gardens to the rear, however, it takes on a very different persona. Here, constant interaction with the natural world is offered via multiple means. Curving walls of glass puncture the concrete framework, opening like lenses to the gardens, while a polished steel screen reflects the greenery in a vivid, almost surreal manner. This part of the house offers a series of terraces and outdoor rooms, as well as a projecting walkway, or 'sky ramp', which cantilevers out from the upper level of

the building, heading towards the treetops, while facing views of the creek. The walkway serves as a floating lookout station for the owners, Rusty and Deedie Rose, who are passionate ornithologists.

'We wanted a place where we could live happily with contemporary art, be able to watch birds in a variety of habitats and have a home that would function as well for an event for three hundred as for two people with two dogs,' Deedie Rose says. 'The most unique quality of the house is the way it unfolds and doesn't reveal itself all at once, and how it integrates into its surroundings, allowing you to see the natural world in new ways.'[46]

Between the two extraordinary elevations, Predock offers a rich variety of spatial, axial and volumetric shifts over three levels. The irregular zigzag pattern of the floorplan fits into the topography of the site, with a double-height atrium, plus circulation and service spaces, towards the centre of the ground storey. The two distinct wings to either side, labelled by the architect as the 'north house' and 'south house', take on a range of functions across the levels,

Above The sky ramp offers a viewing platform up in the treetops for enjoying the wildlife, with the trees mirrored in the surface of the building.

Opposite The house, with its two wings and projecting sky ramp, opens up to the rear garden, where nature rubs up against the architecture.

267

The interiors offer a range of spatial and volumetric experiences arranged around the central, double-height atrium.

but the main focus is on the southern wing, which features the main living spaces at ground level and the master suite above, looking out across the trees. Additional bedrooms are contained in the northern wing, plus a semi-subterranean zone holding additional bedrooms.

Overall, Turtle Creek House offers a purposeful and playful contradiction between mass and transparency, openness and enclosure, as the building unfolds and reveals itself during the journey from the enigmatic entry sequence towards open connectivity with the natural surroundings. Elements such as a curved drum, holding a den on the principal storey and an elevated dining area above, bring additional spatial surprises, while the 1.9 m² (20 sq ft) steel mirror on the

rear elevation, reflecting the trees and the sky ramp, adds to the illusory quality of the building, as the boundaries between architecture and landscape begin to blur.

'There is a purely phenomenological impulse towards the use of that convex mirror – how the light strikes it, and the juxtaposition of this opaque mirror with the transparent yet mirror-like quality of the living-area glazing,' Predock explains. 'Overlaying that intention, however, is the compressed and distorted reflection of the house. This notion of dematerialization and destabilization in a polemical, rather than a perverse way, is part of the intention of the mirrored piece.'[47]

[46] Interview with the author.
[47] Antoine Predock, *Turtle Creek House* (New York: Monacelli Press, 1998).

Left The combined living room and library connect with the back garden via a wall of glass, while the concrete fireplace provides another focal point.

Below The master bedroom on the upper level feels as though it is floating among the trees; the sky ramp can also be seen through the foliage.

House at Toro Canyon

MONTECITO, CALIFORNIA
Barton Myers (1999)

In recent years, the threat of wildfires in California has become increasingly acute – so much so that architects, as well as residents, have been forced to take them into account. Barton Myers now seems prescient in the design of his own family home at Toro Canyon, near Montecito, where the risk of fire was one of the drivers of the design.

Myers and his wife Victoria moved from Toronto to Los Angeles in the 1980s, drawn to the city's architectural projects, as well as by teaching commitments at UCLA. They lived in a Spanish Mission-style house in the Hollywood Hills for a time, but Myers nursed an ambition to build something new. The couple eventually found a forty-acre hillside site bordering the Los Padres National Forest. The beauty of the surroundings was clear, but given the proximity of the forest, so was the risk of wildfires.

Myers decided to work with the landscape and in alliance with nature. Some scrub plants were cleared on the lower hillsides and replaced with groves of orange and olive trees, and the programme was divided into a series of pavilions, on terraces that climb the hillside. This helped to break down the scale and mass of the residence, while forming a quartet of more defensible single-storey structures, tucked into the landscape.

A garage and a separate guest house come first within this ziggurat. Stepping upwards, the main house comes next and then, moving up again, a studio building. Each of these structures (with the exception of the garage) is topped by a pool of water, which helps to insulate and cool the buildings and offers a defence against fire. The water circulates through a pumping system, but this motion is slow, so that the tanks also serve as natural reflecting pools, mirroring the sky, the trees and the buildings themselves.

The house also allowed Myers to explore the use of steel-framed building systems, which have been a regular preoccupation throughout his career. Drawing inspiration from the Case Study masterpieces of Charles and Ray Eames (p. 96), Craig Ellwood (p. 222) and others, he designed a series of steel-framed houses in the US and Canada, of which Toro Canyon House can be seen as the most poetic and accomplished.

Above Water is a key feature in the design, offering a cooling mechanism, reflective surfaces and a valuable reserve for dealing with forest fires.

Opposite The steel-framed master pavilion offers a fluid, double-height living space, with vast winding windows that retract to connect inside and out.

Opposite Airy, spacious and light – the majority of the pavilion is open plan, with a seating area arranged around the fireplace at one end.

Below The kitchen is separated from the dining area and the rest of the pavilion by a partition wall, which also serves as a suitable surface for art.

The main residence is an extraordinary high-tech pavilion in two distinct parts. The front features a double-height super-shed, covered by a steel canopy, which holds the main living space and kitchen, with a triptych of glazed screens that wind upwards, almost like the façade of a fire station. When open, these windows allow for a seamless flow between inside and out; when closed, they create a semi-industrial protective shell for the front elevation. Clerestory windows to the rear bring in added light and offer glimpses of the rising hillside.

The rest of the house is tucked into the slope of the hill. Here, the structure is lower and longer, topped by one of the water pools and holding the bedrooms and ancillary

spaces. Two of these bedrooms project outwards at either end of the floorplan and feature their own winding windows, leading out to adjoining terraces.

Toro Canyon House manages to achieve a balance between openness and protection. It connects with the landscape, while using water as a resource in a way that can be compared with the work of the Australian architect Glenn Murcutt, who has also built in areas of considerable fire risk, using pools as a key element within the integration of architecture, landscaping and nature. Myers's approach serves as a case-study exemplar in itself, offering a way of living that is sensitive to risk, yet is also responsive to the surroundings.

The principal family bedrooms flank the master
pavilion, and benefit from windows front and back
that allow cross-ventilation and instant connectivity
with the landscape.

Tower House

SYRACUSE, NEW YORK
Thomas Gluck / Gluck+ (2012)

Tower House is one in a sequence of distinguished buildings on the Gluck family property in Ulster County, New York. Peter Gluck, the founding partner of architectural firm Gluck+, began the series by extending a cottage from the 1820s, later adding a guest house, called the Bridge House (1996), and the Scholar's Library (2003), a sublime studio for his wife Carol, an expert on modern Japanese history. The latest building, co-designed by Peter Gluck and his son Thomas, represents one of the most dramatic additions to the estate.

When Thomas Gluck decided to build a weekend and holiday home for himself and his family, he was helped by the fact that he already knew this parcel of land intimately. He had spent part of his childhood growing up here, and wanted his own children to enjoy the freedoms offered by this escapist enclave as much as he had. Picking out a favourite spot on an elevated and forested plateau, Gluck came up with the idea of a 'tower' among the trees, one that would make the most of the panoramic view north to the Catskills.

'Accessing the view and creating a living experience up in the treetops became the generator for the whole project,' he explains. 'Looking north towards the mountains, you can see 20 or 25 miles [32 or 40 km] on a clear day – the money shot is the big view.'[48]

Tower House is a striking and unexpected sculpture in the forest, with a tall, vertical shaft climbing upwards and intersected at the fourth storey by an elevated cantilevered box, which holds the main living spaces. Gluck, who first started thinking about the design in 2003, built a full-scale scaffold tower on site before starting construction, to make sure that his ideas would work and the view would be open enough.

The house is accessed via a woodland path leading through the trees and to the base of the tower, which has a modest footprint of around 4 × 11 m (14 × 35 ft). The base is anchored into the bedrock, an idea echoed by the local bluestone pavers in the entrance hallway. The children also have a bedroom on the ground floor, with bespoke bunk beds and storage painted in vibrant yellow. The same colour is used for the custom timber

Above The house offers an enticing belvedere, where the upper level and viewing deck look out across the treetops towards the open landscape.

Opposite The building is clad in clear and coloured glass, which helps to reflect the trees, allowing the house to blur into its woodland setting.

staircase – a playful touch that emphasizes the verticality of the building and the importance of the upward journey. The next two storeys hold the master bedroom and guest rooms on an identical floorplan, with bathrooms alongside within a central core holding all of the plumbing and services.

Climbing upwards again, the house opens into the horizontal living area – the elevated hub of the house. This is a largely open-plan space, arranged around a wood-burning stove, with bespoke window benches to one side and bookcases and storage beneath them. A dining area also sits within this universal space, with the floor and a recess in the ceiling marking out the footprint of the supporting tower.

Left The seating area is arranged around a wood-burning stove; the grey flooring marks the point where the tower meets this elevated piano nobile.

Below The upper level cantilevers out from the tower, creating the a dynamic space with various zones for seating and eating.

The sleeping spaces and the staircase in the tower are enriched with vibrant, playful colours that complement the woodland greenery outside.

Mid-century furniture by Eero Saarinen (p. 120), George Nelson and Hans Wegner is mixed with custom designs, including the dining table. The plywood kitchen, another bespoke design, is the one part of the upper level that can be sealed off with pocket doors. A viewing deck at the top offers an extraordinary platform for drinking in the panorama. The timber and steel-framed tower is completely clad in glass, helping the house to dissolve into the surroundings. Clear-vision glass is used around the main living areas, on the staircase and for edited openings in the bedrooms and bathrooms,

while the rest of the cladding is in opaque 'fritted' glass, which reflects the trees.

'We wanted the building to feel as though it was in the woods, but obviously we have chosen this very artificial and geometric form,' Gluck says. 'One of the under-appreciated aspects of glass is its reflectivity. By having the whole building coated in glass, you reflect everything around it. It becomes this instant camouflage, because you are mirroring the view, so it almost makes the house disappear.'[49]

[48] Interview with the author.
[49] Ibid.

High Desert House

JOSHUA TREE, CALIFORNIA

Kendrick Bangs Kellogg (1993)

The architecture of Kendrick Bangs Kellogg seems to emerge from the ground itself. Buildings like the Onion House in Hawaii and the distinctive 'landscraper' Chart House restaurants in California feel organic, echoing the site-specific sensitivities advocated by Frank Lloyd Wright (p. 54). This is especially true of Kellogg's masterwork in the Joshua Tree National Park, an extraordinary composition that feels both rooted in nature and otherworldly at the same time.

High Desert House was commissioned by the artist Bev Doolittle and her husband Jay. Having taken a series of road trips in the Southwest, where Doolittle began documenting the wilderness and its wildlife, the couple were drawn to Joshua Tree, where they acquired an 'unconventional' site – a raw desert hillside, populated by rocks and boulders. They contacted Kellogg, whose attention was soon captured by the setting.

He developed a series of overlapping concrete canopies, like the segments of a flexible carapace, supported by twenty-six columns that form a layered roofline, enveloping the living spaces below. Accessed by stone steps, the house works around the boulders, with a metal-and-glass doorway resembling the gateway to an ancient fortress. The interiors are protected by the canopies, with glass slotted between them to create an assembly of clerestory windows, giving the house the feeling of something between a nest, a cave and a church.

Given the fluid nature of the internal spaces, off-the-shelf furniture would clearly look out of place. Instead, Kellogg turned to the artist and designer John Vugrin to work on the interiors, which took fifteen years to complete. They had already collaborated on a number of projects, including the Hoshino Wedding Chapel (1988), but High Desert House marked their most complex one yet, with Vugrin designing and making every piece by hand.

His work encompassed major elements like the kitchen and bathrooms, but also other integrated pieces of furniture, including a Kafka-esque dining table, like a multi-legged creature with a tail that curves round and attaches itself to the ceiling. The biomorphic quality of Vugrin's work enhances the idea of

Above The approach to the house feels rather like entering a fortress or bunker, with its processional sequence of steps and a dramatic metal gateway.

Opposite The overlapping plates that shelter the house create a carapace in the rugged landscape, nestling gently among the rocks and boulders.

The biomorphic furniture and lighting installations by John Vugrin took many years to complete; almost every element in the house is bespoke.

an organic *Gesamtkunstwerk*. Vugrin worked on the house until 2014, when the Doolittles moved on and it was acquired by a new owner who fully embraced Kellogg and Vugrin's work.

High Desert House might be compared to the work of the other great American disciples of post-Wright organic architecture, such as John Lautner (p. 210), Bruce Goff (p. 78) and Bart Prince (p. 248). Yet Kellogg seems to take the idea to a new extreme, with 'landscraping' – earthbound buildings, in which the exteriors and interiors fuse to create a fresh hybrid and a new species.

Bedrooms and bathrooms offer contrasts between enclosure and exposure, with the concrete ceiling plates providing protection, while occasional banks of glass connect with the open lunar landscape.

Ex of In House

RHINEBECK, NEW YORK

Steven Holl (2016)

As a contemporary cabin in the woods, Steven Holl's guest house is a delight, but it is also a dynamic architectural experiment. The composition evolved over time through a sequence of drawings and models, exploring the geometrical overlap of four spherical and trapezoidal sections. The house became an 'exploration of in' – a preoccupation of the architect's that has generated a manifesto arguing that 'all space is sacred space'.

The house sits within twenty-eight acres of woodland in Dutchess County, close to a neighbouring farmstead where Holl has made his home for many years. This woodland reserve has become the setting not only for Ex of In, but also a new library and exhibition/event gallery known as Artarc (2019), along with associated buildings and a sculpture trail. Collectively, the compound is known as the 'T' Space Nature Reserve.

The approach to the Ex of In takes visitors past Artarc and through the trees, with the house only revealing itself by degrees. This quiet rural site had been set aside for a subdivision, which could have seen a handful of substantial new residences built here.

Having bought the land, Holl's approach was to preserve its beauty as far as possible. The house, therefore, is modestly scaled, at just 85 m² (918 sq ft), with a low-carbon footprint and net-zero energy consumption. More than this, it is a modern cabin in the woods, which explores complex geometrical intersections.

'We wanted to preserve the landscape,' Holl explains. 'It is a piece of land that was going to be divided into five suburban houses, but we joined the land again and just put one tiny wooden house with four intersecting spheres in the middle.'[50]

The guest house is perched on the brow of a hill, with the woodlands beyond forming a tranquil backdrop and only the sound of the birds and the squirrels at work. The entrance faces eastwards and receives the morning sun, while the southern elevation connects with the light and the trees via two dramatic apertures – one looking out from the seating area over the reflecting pool and frog pond, and the other, on the upper level, a vast oculus that wraps around to the western façade, intersecting with a partial glass floor, which preserves the purity of the sphere.

Above The house explores a range of intersecting geometrical volumes, beginning with the semi-circular bank of glass around the front entrance.

Opposite This experimental building can also be enjoyed as an escapist cabin in the woods, where the natural surroundings have been respected.

Opposite he entrance hall is framed by a crafted sphere (or half-sphere) made from timber, with a step down to the main living space.

Below The kitchen area is a few steps down from the living area; the oculus on the upper level offers a place to appreciate the beauty of the woods.

The front door establishes the spirit of architectural playfulness from the start, set within a semicircular aperture, and framed by the shifting geometry of the rendered eastern elevation. Stepping in, the house unfolds through a series of spatial shifts, forming a kind of topographical journey through a series of interconnected rooms. Once inside, you step down to the double-height living space, illuminated by a large skylight and subtly divided from the kitchen/dining zone by low bookcases and cabinets. A bathroom is hidden away to one side.

The space above this, accessed via the twisting stairway, holds a multi-purpose room that functions both as a bedroom suite, with a Japanese cedar bathtub to one side,

as well as a contemplation space, focused around the large oculus facing the trees. The bedroom also leads through to a small mezzanine sleeping platform, positioned above the entrance and looking down onto the sitting room below.

The interiors of the house have a highly crafted and organic quality, featuring a range of timbers, including mahogany for the window frames, bookcases, kitchen cabinets and stairs, along with birch ply for most of the wall panelling and more curvaceous elements, such as the crafted hallway. The use of plywood offers continuity and cohesion, while allowing the complex geometry of the spaces to come together and unify.

Below The various levels of the house can be best seen from the main seating area; the kitchen is on the lower level, with the sleeping zone at the top.

Opposite The bedroom connects with the landscape via a window to one side, as well as the oculus, which can be seen from the bed.

As with so much of Holl's work, the house explores complex geometrical intersections, offering a series of contrasts between spheres and rectangles, diagonals and straight lines, all within a modest footprint and floorplan. This is certainly a house of ideas, but it is also a Walden-esque cabin to enjoy and nest inside, providing a place for connecting with the character of the house, and with the landscape around it.

'I am excited that people love to stay here,' Holl says. 'The views of the trees through small, focused window openings, the natural light, the silence, are all deeply gratifying. It is a kind of belvedere, but it's not just about viewing – the light and the silence are also central to the experience of being here.'[51]

[50] Diana Carta, *Lake of the Mind: A Conversation with Steven Holl* (Siracusa, Italy: LetteraVentidue, 2018).
[51] Interview with the author.

Woodstock Vermont Farm

WOODSTOCK, VERMONT

Rick Joy (2008)

Architect Rick Joy grew up in the northeastern state of Maine, but is associated with the Southwest, particularly Arizona, where his studio is based and many of his early projects are located. New England represents a very different context, but when invited to design a 21st-century farmstead in Vermont for a real-estate developer and his family, Joy embraced the challenge.

'When I left Maine to study architecture, I had every intention of returning,' he explains. 'I fell for "the other", as they say, yet dreamed of coming back to build. My client took the first step, and said: "I want to be the one to bring you home".'[52]

The site sits within 210 acres of farmland and woods, not far from the town of Woodstock. The setting is rural and peaceful, with the trees offering a soft backdrop that changes with the seasons. The new farmhouse and its companion barn sit alongside a spring-fed pond within a natural bowl in the landscape. The farmhouse replaces an old cottage, while a remaining shed by the pond, along with remnants of stone field walls, offer reminders of the past.

The considered composition of farmhouse and barn echoes vernacular tradition, even though the outline of the two buildings are distinctly contemporary.

The main house is, in Joy's words, 'a loaf of bread' – a long house with a slim, elegant presence in the landscape. Coated in cedar shingles, the house has two stone gables, made from characterful Lake Champlain bedrock. One of these holds the main entrance, or 'maze', which offers a process of discovery as one steps through an enigmatic open doorway in the stonework, before following the path around to the front door.

Beyond the entrance hall and the neat mud room alongside it, the steel-framed farmhouse opens up dramatically. Here, the great room – an open-plan space with a double-height, pitched ceiling – features a seating area arranged around the stone fireplace, a dining area towards the centre and an open kitchen beyond. The wooden floors, walls and ceiling create a highly organic quality, while a bank of sliding glass to one side frames a view of the pond, the meadow alongside it and the woods.

Above The long house balances the use of stone and shingles with a maze-like entrance and end gable picked out in characterful stonework.

Opposite The house and barn nearby work in synergy, with the two distinctive forms creating a farmstead arranged around a spring-fed pond.

THE WHOLE YEAR INN

A hidden service core includes a pantry and steps down to the basement, beyond which are three bedrooms. At the far end of the house is the master suite, with its own fireplace set into the gable wall. The bedroom also offers a soaring ceiling height, with space for a bathtub, facing the view; a separate bathroom has a shower area with a double enclosure. The long gallery running along one side of the house connects these spaces together and features a series of

The great room is a generous space with high ceilings and a crafted character all of its own; the space includes a kitchen, dining area and seating zone, arranged around a stone fireplace.

The long hallway to one side of the house connects the living spaces within one neat axial line; the master suite is at the opposite end of the house to the great room and has a fireplace of its own, set into the stone gable end.

distinctive cut-out windows; a desk and study space are also tucked within the inner wall of the gallery. Highly crafted detailing includes custom leather door pulls in place of handles.

The overall impression is one of a generosity of space, with one's eye constantly drawn out to the surrounding landscape. There is a wealth of integrated storage, allowing the living area and bedrooms to remain uncluttered and preserve the luxury of open living. The substantial basement holds further storage rooms and an indoor hockey rink, while the house is heated by a geothermal system, with the temperature regulated by structural insulated panels.

The barn is also shingle-coated, but has a more agricultural feel. Inside, the lower level contains garaging, storage and services, while upstairs is a 'loft hall', with bedrooms, bunk rooms and bathrooms to either side. The barn leads out to a deck that cantilevers over the pond, which becomes a reflecting pool, mirroring the trees and farm buildings.

'It was a dream project for us,' says the client. 'Our wish was to create a modern home that was also informal and relaxed. "Pure joy" sums up who designed it, what it is and how it is experienced.'[53]

[52] Interview with the author.
[53] Ibid.

The Pierre

SAN JUAN ISLANDS, WASHINGTON

Tom Kundig / Olson Kundig (2010)

Above The house burrows into the landscape, with a terrace sitting to one side, providing a partially sheltered outdoor room.

Opposite Covered by a green roof, the house becomes part of the topography, creating the lightest possible impact on this mesmerizing coastal landscape.

As a student at the University of Washington, architect Tom Kundig began by studying geophysics, following his own fascination with geology and tectonics. It was only later that he decided to switch his focus to architecture, yet this preoccupation with elemental forces and the way they shaped the landscape remained with him.

Many of Kundig's residential projects have explored the relationship between architecture and the rural landscape, taking a highly contextual approach to settings and surroundings. But The Pierre, located among the San Juan Islands, in the borderland between Washington State and Canada, takes this relationship to a new level. The house is pushed into the rocky topography, creating an extraordinary synergy between the natural and the artificial.

'Putting the house in the rock follows a tradition of building on the least productive part of a site, leaving the best parts for cultivation,' he explains. 'The decision to engage with the site was a natural evolution of that idea. Whenever you work with natural materials, it becomes a reciprocal

relationship. We knew it was a possibility the rock might fracture in ways we didn't want, so we had to be nimble with our design and accept that things might change.'[54]

Kundig had known the client, an art collector, for many years. She had owned the coastal site for some time, and asked Kundig to create a modestly scaled retreat for herself, her family and friends, as well as a canvas for her collections of art, sculpture and furniture. The rocky outcrop, or hillock, was always one of her favourite spots, offering a slightly elevated position and an open vista of the Salish Sea. By drilling down into the outcrop, The Pierre – meaning 'stone' – became a halfway house between a cave and a belvedere, exploring the juxtaposition between mass and transparency.

'The house is orientated to frame the view of the water, as well as of the landscape,' Kundig adds. 'The position also responds to the very human desire to be able to survey your surroundings while feeling safe. The contrast between mass and transparency became the principal driver of the design, with the solidity of the rock becoming the yin

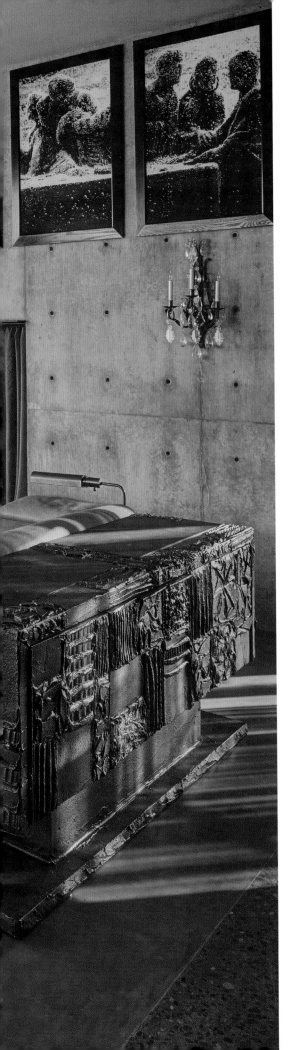

to the transparency of the house – the yang. We wanted the nature of the site to dominate and so the house is embraced by the stone.'[55]

The majority of the house is arranged across a single level, accessed via a narrow alleyway partly cut into the rock, creating a processional entrance that is also enigmatic, heightening the sense of expectation. The entry area within is bordered by a small powder room with a particularly cave-like quality, with sunlight provided only by a light tube drilled into the ceiling. This entrance sequence is sheltered by an internal wall of recycled timber, which also hides utility spaces behind pivoting bookshelves, before emerging from the rear of the house in the form of a crafted timber storage pod.

The central, open-plan living area is largely concentrated on the view out across the water, yet the integrated fireplace also offers another key focal point for the seating area.

Opposite The master bedroom connects with the terrace alongside, while also benefiting from the framed view out across the sound.

Below Situated alongside the main entrance, the powder room is a cave-like space drilled into the rock and illuminated by solar tubes.

The main living area is at the heart of the plan, sitting on an axis that runs right through the rocky outcrop, with walls of glass at the front and back. This space has been zoned with areas devoted to the kitchen/breakfast area, a dining table at the centre and a seating zone placed for the best of the views and access to the open fire, where the base of the hearth is formed from another stump of rock. A master suite sits to one side, with a modest guest bedroom alongside; another guest room is positioned separately on a lower level. There is also access from the main living space – via a vast, pivoting glass door – to a partially sheltered terrace, perched upon the stone, complete with an outdoor fireplace. This serves as a

gently elevated outdoor room, perfect for appreciating the vista and the natural beauty of the surroundings.

In some respects, The Pierre recalls the work of modernist masters such as John Lautner, whose Elrod House (1968; p. 210) in Palm Springs was famously woven into a rocky cliffside. There are parallels, too, with Albert Frey's House II (1964; p. 226), also in Palm Springs, which explores similar contrasts between openness and enclosure, mass and transparency, but on a smaller scale. For a building created on a relatively modest footprint, The Pierre also has a powerful sense of resonance and depth.

[54] Interview with the author.
[55] Ibid.

Biographies

Welton Becket (1902–1969)

Born in Seattle, Welton Becket moved to Los Angeles in 1933, where he formed a partnership with Charles Plummer and Walter Wurdeman. In 1949, following the deaths of both colleagues, the practice was renamed Welton Becket & Associates. As well as many residential commissions, Becket's key projects included Capitol Records Building in Hollywood (1956), Los Angeles International Airport (1959; with William Pereira and others) and the Los Angeles Music Center (1964).

Marcel Breuer (1902–1981)

Born in Hungary, Marcel Breuer studied at the Bauhaus in Weimar and, after graduation in 1924, became a junior master at the Bauhaus Dessau and director of the furniture workshop. In 1928 Breuer opened his own architectural practice in Berlin, but moved to Budapest in 1933 and, two years later, to London, where he formed a brief partnership with F.R.S. Yorke and developed an innovative series of plywood furniture for Isokon. In 1937, he accepted an invitation from his former Bauhaus colleague and mentor Walter Gropius (p. 48) to teach at Harvard, while also forming a joint architectural practice. Following the dissolution of this partnership, Breuer opened an office in New York in 1946 and embarked on a series of residential and other projects, including the Whitney Museum of American Art (1966).

Ogden Codman, Jr (1863–1951)

Architect and designer Ogden Codman, Jr was born in Massachusetts and studied at MIT, yet spent much of his formative years in France, which was to become a constant influence on his life and work. He launched his own architectural practice in 1891, initially based in Boston and then New York. Following the success of The Mount and The Decoration of Houses, he went on to design for many prestigious clients, including John D. Rockefeller, Jr and Frederick William Vanderbilt. In 1920, Codman, like Edith Wharton before him, settled in France.

Charles Deaton (1921–1996)

Born in New Mexico, Charles Deaton was a self-educated architect and designer. During the Second World War he worked for Lockheed, before moving to New York and then St Louis. He settled in Colorado in the 1950s, and began specializing in the design of banks, including the Central Bank & Trust building (1960) and the Key Savings & Loan (1967), both in Colorado, and the Wyoming National Bank (1964). He was also known for his stadium designs, including the adjacent Arrowhead and Kauffman stadiums (1972) in Kansas City, Missouri. He designed furniture, lighting and several patented board games.

Alden B. Dow (1904–1983)

Born in Midland, Michigan, Alden B. Dow studied architecture at Columbia University, graduating in 1931. He served an apprenticeship with the Saginaw-based firm Frantz & Spence, and then joined the Taliesen Fellowship in early 1933. Returning to Michigan, Dow established his own architectural practice in 1933, beginning with the design of his own studio (p. 66). A few years later, he received a Diplome de Grand Prix at the 1937 Paris International Exposition for his design of the John Whitman Residence in Midland, built with Dow's patented Unit Blocks. He went on to design houses, churches, commercial and civic buildings in Michigan and beyond, including the Grace A. Dow Memorial Library (1953) and the Midland Center for the Arts (1968).

Tony Duquette (1914–1999)

Born in Los Angeles, Tony Duquette studied at the city's Chouinard Art Institute and at the Yale School of Drama. His career began with work as an in-house designer for Bullock's department store, followed by freelance work for celebrated interior designer William Haines. Later, he was 'discovered' by the influential interior decorator Elsie de Wolfe, who championed his work and commissioned pieces of furniture. Duquette opened his own studio in 1941, and, as well as interiors, furniture and jewelry design, he also had a successful career as a set decorator for film and theatre.

Charles (1907–1978) & Ray Eames (1912–1988)

Born in St Louis, Missouri, Charles Eames won an architecture scholarship to Washington University. He practised architecture during the 1930s, before taking up a fellowship at Cranbrook Academy of Art, where he met artist Ray Kaiser; the couple were married in 1941. They moved to Los Angeles, with Charles initially working in the art department at MGM and Ray designing magazine covers for *Arts & Architecture* magazine. Their innovative designs in plywood during the 1940s helped provide the impetus to launch their multi-disciplinary studio. Key designs, including the 'LCW' (1946), 'La Chaise' (1948) and '670 Lounge' (1956) chairs, are still produced by Herman Miller and Vitra.

Caspar Ehmcke (1908–1995)

Caspar Ehmcke was born in Munich, Germany, and went on to study at the Stuttgart Technical University. In 1933, he emigrated to America and settled in Los Angeles. His American career began with planning work for a number of department stores, including Bullock's, which also employed Tony Duquette. During the war years, his projects included a test facility for the US Navy. In 1945 Ehmcke launched his own architectural practice in Los Angeles, specializing in residential design, as well as occasional commercial commissions, such as a recording studio for Decca records.

Peter Eisenman (b. 1932)

Born in New Jersey, Peter Eisenman studied at Cornell and Columbia, and at Cambridge in the UK. Along with Michael Graves, John Hejduk, Charles Gwathmey (p. 204) and Richard Meier (p. 230), he was one of an experimental group of neo- and postmodernists called the 'New York Five', a term coined by Philip Johnson (p. 102).

He worked as an independent architect, academic and theorist, before founding Eisenman Architects in 1980. Key projects include the Memorial to the Murdered Jews of Europe (2006), Berlin, and the University of Phoenix Stadium (2006) in Glendale, Arizona.

Craig Ellwood (1922–1992)

Born Jon Nelson Burke in Texas, Craig Ellwood enlisted in the US Army Air Corps during the Second World War, and later worked as a cost estimator in the construction industry while taking evening classes in architecture, engineering and design. He set up Craig Ellwood Associates in Los Angeles in 1948 and after meeting John Entenza, editor of *Arts & Architecture* magazine and pioneer of the Case Study programme, went on to design three exemplary houses. An expert in steel-frame construction techniques, Ellwood designed a series of innovation residential pavilions across California over the following years.

Joseph Esherick (1914–1998)

After serving an apprenticeship with his uncle, the artist and furniture-maker Wharton Esherick (p. 30), Joseph Esherick studied architecture at the University of Pennsylvania in his home city of Philadelphia. He served in the US Navy during the Second World War and opened his own practice in San Francisco in 1946; from 1952 onwards he also taught at UC Berkeley. Along with the residences at Sea Ranch, Esherick also designed many other private homes. Key projects include The Cannery (1968) in San Francisco, and Wurster Hall (1964) at UC Berkeley, home of the College of Environmental Design, which Esherick co-founded.

Wharton Esherick (1887–1970)

Artist, sculptor and designer Wharton Esherick was born in Philadelphia, Pennsylvania, first learning woodworking at the city's Manual Training High School. He went on to study printmaking, drawing and painting at the Philadelphia Museum and School of Industrial Art and the Pennsylvania Academy of Fine Arts. His career began with carved, decorative wooden picture frames, followed by woodcut prints and book illustration, and finally sculpture, furniture and interiors. Interior commissions included the Curtis Bok House (1937) in Gulph Mills, and the kitchen at the house designed by Louis Kahn for his niece, Margaret Esherick (1961; p. 156).

Richard Foster (1919–2002)

Born in Pittsburgh, Pennsylvania, Richard Foster studied architecture at the Pratt Institute. Graduating in 1950, he went to work for Philip Johnson (p. 102) and contributed to many of Johnson's projects during the 1960s and '70s, including the New York State Pavilion for the 1964 World's Fair in New York and the New York State Theater (1964; now known as the David H. Koch Theater) at Lincoln Center. Foster continued working with Johnson even after forming his own practice, Richard Foster Associates. His most famous solo project remains the Round House.

Albert Frey (1903–1998)

Born in Zurich, Switzerland, Albert Frey studied at the Winterthur Institute of Technology. He worked in Brussels and then in Paris, where he found a position in Le Corbusier's office, assisting with the design of Villa Savoye (1931). Frey emigrated to America in 1930, working in New York, before eventually settling in Palm Springs in 1939. Many of Frey's most distinctive and best-known projects are located in and around Palm Springs, including many mid-century modern residences, and larger buildings such as the Palm Springs Desert Museum (1953), Palm Springs City Hall (1957) and Tramway Gas Station (1965).

Andrew Geller (1924–2011)

Born in Brooklyn, New York, Andrew Geller studied architecture at Cooper Union and served in the US Army Corps of Engineers during the Second World War. Some years later, he joined the multi-disciplinary design studio Raymond Loewy Associates, where he worked for the next three decades, becoming head of the architecture department. Projects include department stores, shopping centres and the interiors of Lever House (1952) by Skidmore, Owings & Merrill, along with designs for pre-fabricated holiday homes, including 200 houses at Leisurama, in Montauk, New York. Geller is best known for a series of highly individual vacation houses built on Long Island during the 1950s and '60s, designed on a freelance basis.

Thomas Gluck

Thomas Gluck studied at Harvard and Yale, before joining Herzog & de Meuron, where he worked on their design for the Walker Art Center in Minneapolis. In 2006 he joined Peter Gluck & Partners, founded by his father in 1972, and became a principal at the practice, which was renamed Gluck+. His projects include the The Stack (2014), a residential project in New York, and The Bridge residential scheme in Philadelphia (2017).

Bruce Goff (1904–1982)

Born in Kansas, Bruce Goff moved a number of times during his childhood, from Oklahoma to Colorado, and back to Tulsa. Having shown a talent for drawing from a young age, he secured an apprenticeship with the Tulsa-based architectural practice Rush, Endacott & Rush at the age of just twelve. He followed the advice of his mentor Frank Lloyd Wright (p. 54) and learned his craft at the drawing board, rather than going to an architectural school. He served in the Naval Construction branch of the US Navy during the Second World War, and taught at the University of Oklahoma until 1955. Residential projects include Ledbetter House (1947) and Bavinger House (1950), both in Norman, Oklahoma, and the Pavilion for Japanese Art at the Los Angeles County Museum of Art, completed posthumously by Goff's student Bart Prince (p. 248) in 1978.

Charles (1868–1957) & Henry Greene (1870–1954)

The most accomplished and influential proponents of the Arts & Crafts style in the US, brothers Charles and Henry Greene were born near Cincinnati, Ohio, and studied in St Louis and then at MIT in Cambridge, Massachusetts. In 1893, the brothers moved to Pasadena, California, and established their own architectural practice a year later; much of their subsequent residential work is located in California. In 1916, Charles Greene moved to Carmel, while Henry remained focused on the practice in Pasadena. Their joint practice dissolved in 1922, with the two brothers undertaking solo projects in later years.

Walter Gropius (1883–1969)
Born in Berlin, Walter Gropius worked in the office of Peter Behrens, before founding his own practice in 1910. Following military service during the First World War, he became director of the Bauhaus, and in 1925 masterminded the school's move to Dessau, where he also opened an architectural practice and designed many buildings for the new campus. Gropius stepped down as director in 1928 and moved to England in 1934, opening a new office with Maxwell Fry. Three years later, he moved to the US, becoming director of the Department of Architecture at Harvard in 1938. From 1938 to 1941 he worked in practice with Marcel Breuer (p. 192). Gropius's most famous building in the US is the Pan Am Building (1963) in New York.

Charles Gwathmey (1938–2009)
Born in Charlotte, North Carolina, Charles Gwathmey studied architecture at the University of Pennsylvania and at Yale and worked in the New York office of Edward Larrabee Barnes, before concentrating on a commission to build a house for his parents. Known as one of the 'New York Five' – along with Peter Eisenman (p. 236), Richard Meier (p. 230), Michael Graves and John Hejduk – he formed Gwathmey Siegel & Associates with Robert Siegel in 1968. He designed houses for well-known clients, including Steven Spielberg, and a number of museums, including the American Museum of the Moving Image (1982) and an addition to the Guggenheim Museum (1992), both in New York.

Steven Holl (b. 1947)
After studying architecture at the University of Washington, Steven Holl continued his education in Rome and at the Architectural Association in London. He founded in his own practice in New York in 1976, and teaches at Columbia University. Key projects include Simmons Hall (2002) at MIT, in Cambridge, Massachusetts, the Bloch Building (2007) at the Nelson-Atkins Museum of Art in Kansas City, and innovative residences such as Turbulence House (2005) in New Mexico and the Y-House (1999) in the Catskills, New York.

Philip Johnson (1906–2005)
Born in Cleveland, Ohio, Philip Johnson studied at Harvard, before joining the Museum of Modern Art, New York, in 1930 as a curator, where his most influential contribution was the International Style exhibition in 1932. Later, he returned to Harvard to study architecture under Walter Gropius (p. 48) and Marcel Breuer (p. 192). Johnson collaborated with Ludwig Mies van der Rohe (p. 108) on the design of the Seagram Building and Four Seasons restaurant (1959) and designed a number of innovative residences during the mid-century period. Later projects included the AT&T Building (1984) in New York.

A. Quincy Jones (1913–1979)
Born in Kansas City, Archibald Quincy Jones studied architecture at the University of Washington and worked for several architectural practices in California, before serving in the US Navy during the war. In 1945, he opened his own practice in Los Angeles and collaborated with architects such as Frederick Emmons. Jones designed condominiums, hotels, academic buildings and tract houses, including large-scale projects with the developer Joseph Eichler. Key projects include Jones's own residence, The Barn (1950), in Los Angeles, and the USC Annenberg School for Communications (1976–9). He also taught at the USC School of Architecture.

Rick Joy (b. 1958)
Rick Joy studied music at the University of Maine, followed by sculpture and photography at the Portland School of Art. After moving to Tucson, Arizona, in 1985, he began studying architecture at the University of Arizona, and worked in the office of William Bruder, as well as designing and building his own family home in Tucson. Rick Joy Architect was launched in 1993; the firm is also known as Studio Rick Joy. Key residential projects include Tubac House (2000), Tucson Mountain House (2001) and Desert Nomad House (2004), all in Arizona; other work includes the Amangiri hotel (2009) in Utah and Princeton Transit Hall & Market (2018).

Louis Kahn (1901–1974)
Louis Kahn was born in Estonia and emigrated to Philadelphia in 1906, when he was just five years old, becoming a US citizen in 1915. After studying architecture at the University of Pennsylvania, he worked for a number of local practices, embarked on a formative tour of Europe in 1928 and established his own practice in Philadelphia in 1934. Having focused on residential projects, in the postwar period he worked on increasingly complex and ambitious projects, including the Salk Institute (1965) in San Diego, the Kimbell Art Museum (1972) in Fort Worth, Texas, and the National Parliament complex in Dhaka, Bangladesh, which was finally completed in 1982.

Ray Kappe (b. 1927)
Ray Kappe and his family moved from Minneapolis, where he was born, to Los Angeles in 1940. He served in the US Army Corp of Engineers during the Second World War, and then studied architecture at UC Berkeley, where tutors included the modernist master Erich Mendelsohn. After working as a draughtsman on the development of Eichler tract homes, Kappe founded his own practice in the mid-1950s. Over the following decades, he designed around 100 contextual residences, which responded to the rugged topography in and around Los Angeles. Kappe taught at Cal Poly before co-founding SCI-Arc in 1972.

Kendrick Bangs Kellogg (b. 1934)
Born in San Diego, Kendrick Bangs Kellogg studied mathematics, engineering and design at San Diego State, the University of Colorado, USC and UC Berkeley. A meeting

with Frank Lloyd Wright (p. 54) confirmed his passion for organic architecture, although he did not take up a Taliesen Fellowship. One of his first completed buildings was the Onion House (1962) in Hawaii. After obtaining his architect's license in California in 1964, he went on to design a series of residences, including Surfer House (1973) in La Jolla, and a collection of characterful Chart House restaurants. Overseas, Kellogg completed the Hoshino Chapel in Karuizawa, Japan, in 1988.

Tom Kundig (b. 1954)
Born in California, Tom Kundig grew up in Spokane, Washington, where his father was an architect. He studied architecture at the University of Washington and became a partner at Olson Kundig Architects, based in Seattle, in 1994; the firm now has five partners, including original founder Jim Olson. Kundig's projects include Montecito Residence (2007), Rolling Huts (2007), Studhorse (2012) and the Tacoma Art Museum (2014).

John Lautner (1911–1994)
Born in Michigan, John Lautner took a degree in English before beginning a Taliesin apprenticeship with Frank Lloyd Wright (p. 54). After six years working with Wright, Lautner launched his own practice in California in 1940, with a focus on residential projects. Much of his work over the following decades was located in and around Hollywood, Beverly Hills and other Los Angeles neighbourhoods, with the work becoming increasingly expressive and dynamic. Key projects include Malin House (1960; known as 'Chemosphere'), Garcia House (1962) and – further afield – Arango Residence (1973) in Acapulco, Mexico.

Ricardo Legorreta (1931–2011)
Born in Mexico City, Ricardo Legorreta studied architecture at the Universidad Nacional Autónoma de México. He worked with José Villagrán García's practice for ten years before establishing his own atelier in 1963; in 2000, Legorreta's son Victor became a partner and the firm was renamed Legorreta + Legorreta. As well as working across Mexico, Legorreta also worked across Latin America

and in the US. Key projects included the seminal Camino Real Hotel (1968) in Mexico City, the Museo de Arte Contemporáneo (1991) in Monterrey, the Metropolitan Cathedral (1993) in Managua and the San Antonio Public Library (1995). He was awarded the Praemium Imperiale architectural prize just before his death in 2011.

David Leavitt (1918–2013)
David Leavitt studied at the University of Nebraska and worked, during the summer months, with Antonin Raymond, who had worked for Frank Lloyd Wright (p. 54) in Japan before founding his own practice. Following service in the US Navy during the Second World War, Leavitt rejoined Raymond, working on projects in both America and Japan. In the mid-1950s, Leavitt founded his own practice, concentrating largely on residential projects, which took inspiration from Japanese architecture and interiors.

Richard Meier (b. 1934)
Born in Newark, New Jersey, Richard Meier studied architecture at Cornell, before working in the New York office of Marcel Breuer for three years. He launched his own practice in New York in 1963, and was one of the 'New York Five', along with his contemporaries Peter Eisenman (p. 236), Charles Gwathmey (p. 204), Michael Graves and John Hejduk. From early residential commissions, Meier progressed to an international portfolio of museums and galleries, including the Frankfurt Museum of Decorative Arts (1985), the Barcelona Museum of Contemporary Art (1995) and the Getty Center (1997) in Los Angeles.

Ludwig Mies van der Rohe (1886–1969)
Born in Aachen, Mies van der Rohe trained as a draughtsman before moving to Berlin. He worked for Peter Behrens from 1908 until 1913, when he started his own architectural practice, which was interrupted by military service during the First World War. In 1929 he designed the German Pavilion at the Barcelona Universal Exhibition, and became the director of the Bauhaus in 1930. Mies emigrated to America in 1938, becoming the

director of the Armour Institute of Technology (later Illinois Institute of Technology) in Chicago, and establishing an office in the city. He became a US citizen in 1944. Key projects include the Lake Shore Drive Apartments (1951) in Chicago and the Seagram Building (1958) in New York.

Barton Myers (b. 1934)
Born in Norfolk, Virginia, Barton Myers studied attended the US Naval Academy in Annapolis, Maryland. Following his military service, he studied architecture at the University of Pennsylvania and worked in the office of Louis Kahn (p. 156) in Philadelphia for two years. In 1968 he founded his own practice in Toronto, Canada, which has been based since 1984 in Los Angeles, where Myers has taught at the UCLA School of Architecture since 1980. Key projects include Wolf House (1974) in Toronto, the Seagram Museum (1983) in Waterloo, Ontario, and the Cerritos Center for the Performing Arts (1993) in California.

George Nakashima (1905–1990)
Born in Spokane, Washington, George Nakashima studied architecture at the University of Washington and at MIT. In 1931 he began working in Japan with Antonin Raymond, and from 1937 to 1939 oversaw the construction of an ashram dormitory in Pondicherry, India, designed by Raymond. In 1942, Nakashima and his family were interred in Idaho, where he worked with master craftsman Gentaro Hilkogawa. With Raymond's help, Nakashima left the camp in 1943 and settled in New Hope, Pennsylvania, where he began creating his distinctive handcrafted furniture, including designs for Knoll and Widdicomb.

Richard Neutra (1892–1970)
Born in Vienna, Richard Neutra studied architecture under Adolf Loos, and after military service during the First World War, worked with Erich Mendelsohn in Berlin. Emigrating to the US in 1923, he worked briefly with Frank Lloyd Wright (p. 54) and collaborated with friend and colleague Rudolph Schindler (p. 26), before establishing

his own practice in Los Angeles. An early project, Lovell Health House (1929) in Los Angeles, provided a catalyst for a wave of residential commissions. During the 1950s, Neutra began to work on his own projects in the US and in his later years completed houses in France, Germany and Switzerland.

Oscar Niemeyer (1907–2012)

One of the most influential modernist architects, Oscar Niemeyer was born in Rio de Janeiro, where he studied architecture at the National Art Academy. In 1934 he joined Lúcio Costa's team working with Le Corbusier on a new building for the Ministry of Education and Health in Rio, and in 1940 secured a commission for the Pampulha complex in Belo Horizonte. During the 1950s, he was appointed chief architect for the new capital of Brasília, where his buildings include the Metropolitan Cathedral and the National Congress. In 1964 he went into political exile in France, returning to Brazil in 1982. Niemeyer was awarded the Pritzker Prize in 1988.

William Pereira (1909–1985)

Born in Chicago, William Pereira studied architecture at the University of Illinois. He worked briefly with Holabird & Root in Chicago, before founding his own practice in Los Angeles in 1931; during the 1950s there was also a partnership with architect Charles Luckman. As well as private residences, Pereira designed libraries, art centres, banks and commercial buildings. Key projects include the Los Angeles County Museum of Art (1964), the Transamerica Pyramid building (1972) in San Francisco and the Geisel Library (1970) at UC San Diego. Pereira also enjoyed a parallel career in the 1940s as a Hollywood art director.

Antoine Predock (B. 1936)

Born in Lebanon, Missouri, Antoine Predock studied at the University of New Mexico and at Colombia. In 1967 he established his own practice in Albuquerque, with the native landscape forming a key part of his highly contextual version of 'portable regionalism'. Many of his early projects were in New

Mexico, including La Luz Townhouses (1970) in Albuquerque and House in the Sandia Mountains (1977). Key projects include the American Heritage Center (1993) in Wyoming, the Tacoma Art Museum (2003) in Washington, and San Diego Padres Petco Park (2004). Predock was awarded a Gold Medal by the American Institute of Architects in 2006.

Bart Prince (B. 1947)

Bart Prince was born in Albuquerque, New Mexico, where he established his own practice in 1973. He studied architecture at Arizona State University where he first met Bruce Goff (p. 78), whose organic approach was – in turn – influenced by the work of Frank Lloyd Wright (p. 54). Prince worked intermittently with his mentor over a number of years and after his death, went on to complete Goff's work on the Pavilion for Japanese Art (1978–88) at the Los Angeles County Museum of Art. Many of his residential projects are located in the southwestern United States, including his own residence and studio in Albuquerque (1984).

Paul Rudolph (1918–1997)

Although Paul Rudolph spent little more than a decade living and working in Florida, he is seen as a key figure of the Sarasota School of Architecture. Born in Kentucky, he studied at Auburn University and at Harvard, where he was taught by Walter Gropius (p. 48). A partnership with Ralph Twitchell (p. 84) lasted from 1941 to 1951, when he began his own practice. Rudolph designed the Art and Architecture Building at Yale (1963) and served as chair of the Architecture Department for six years. Other projects include Milam House (1961) in Jacksonville, Florida, and the Rudolph Penthouse and Apartments (1982) in New York.

Eero Saarinen (1910–1961)

The son of architect and educator Eliel Saarinen (p. 36), Eero Saarinen was born in Finland and moved with his family to the US in 1923. He studied architecture at Yale and, after travels in Europe, began working for Eliel Saarinen's practice, based in Michigan; father and son completed a number of

significant projects together during the 1940s. Following his father's death in 1950, Saarinen launched Eero Saarinen & Associates. Key buildings include the TWA Terminal (1962) at JFK Airport in New York, the North Christian Church (1963) in Columbus, Indiana, and the American Embassy (1960) in London. He also designed many innovative pieces of furniture for Knoll, including the famous 'Tulip' chair (1956).

Eliel Saarinen (1873–1950)

Born in Rantasalmi, Finland, Eliel Saarinen studied at Helsinki University, where he first met Herman Gesellius and Armas Lindgren, who became his partners in 1897. The trio worked on a number of projects, including the Finnish Pavilion for the 1900 World's Fair in Paris, Helsinki Railway Station (1906) and the Finnish National Museum (1910). Saarinen also designed a family home at Hvitträsk in 1902. In 1923, he emigrated to the US. He began working at Cranbrook Academy of Art in 1925, becoming its president in 1932. During the 1930s and '40s, Saarinen worked in private practice with his son, Eero Saarinen (p. 120).

George Sanderson, Jr (1906–1959)

Born in Massachusetts, George Sanderson, Jr studied at Groton School and then Yale, where he was a contemporary of George Morris. He went on to complete his studies at MIT, and worked in both Los Angeles and Boston. During the Second World War he served in the Office of War Information and later became an architectural writer, based in New York, including a position as features editor, from 1955 onwards, of *Progressive Architecture* magazine.

Rudolph Schindler (1887–1953)

Born in Vienna, Austria, Rudolph Schindler attended the city's University of Technology, followed by the Academy of Fine Arts, studying under Otto Wagner, Adolf Loos and Carl König; he also first met Richard Neutra (p. 72) in 1912. Schindler emigrated to America in 1914, working initially with the Chicago practice Ottenheimer, Stern & Reichert, before securing a position in the office of Frank Lloyd Wright (p. 54) from 1918 onwards.

Wright asked Schindler to relocate to Los Angeles in 1920 to supervise the construction of the Hollyhock House, and he established his own practice in the city two years later. Key projects include Lovell Beach House (1922) in Newport Beach, and Fitzpatrick House (1936) in the Hollywood Hills.

John Butler Swann, Jr (1903–1997)

Born in Pittsfield, Massachusetts, as a child John Butler Swann lived at different times in Boston and the Berkshires region of Massachusetts, New York, Virginia and Costa Rica. He went to school in Concord, New Hampshire, and in Switzerland, before studying at Harvard; he also attended the Beacon Hill School of Design in 1932. In the mid-1930s he began farming in the Berkshires, but also undertook design projects for friends and acquaintances, including George Morris and Suzy Frelinghuysen (p. 60).

Ralph Twitchell (1890–1978)

Born in Ohio, Ralph Twitchell moved to Florida as a teenager and studied at Rollins College in Orlando and McGill University, Montreal, before graduating from Colombia. He served as an aviator during the First World War, followed by an apprenticeship in New York, and settled in Sarasota after being asked to oversee the construction of a house for the Ringling family, designed by Dwight James Baum. Twitchell opened his own practice in Sarasota in 1936, and formed a partnership with Paul Rudolph (p. 126) that lasted from 1941 to 1951. Key projects include the Twitchell Residence (1941), Miller Residence (1948) and Burnette Residence (1950).

Simon Ungers (1957–2006)

Architect and artist Simon Ungers was the son of the celebrated German architect O.M. Ungers, and came to America in 1969, when his father was appointed chair of the department of architecture at Cornell (where he himself would graduate from in 1980). In 1984, he formed an architectural practice with Laszlo Kiss and Todd Zwigard, known as UKZ Design. Many of Ungers's projects were residential, yet explored ideas of abstraction within striking and sculptural compositions.

These include the Knee Residence (1984) in Caldwell, New Jersey, and Cube House (2001) in Ithaca, New York. From 2000, Ungers worked increasingly in Cologne, Germany, where he was born.

Robert Venturi (1925–2018)

An architect, writer, teacher and theorist, Robert Venturi's ideas were as important as his buildings. Born in Philadelphia, he studied at Princeton, before working briefly with Eero Saarinen (p. 120) and in the Philadelphia office of Louis Kahn (p. 156). He met his wife Denise Scott Brown while teaching at the University of Pennsylvania, and they formed their own practice in 1969. Notable buildings include the Sainsbury Wing (1991) of the National Gallery, London, and the Seattle Art Museum (1991). Their book *Learning from Las Vegas* (1972) is widely seen as the unofficial manifesto of Postmodernism.

Edith Wharton (1862–1937)

Wharton is best known, of course, as a novelist and writer; among her many books are literary classics such as *The House of Mirth* (1905) and *The Age of Innocence* (1920), which won the Pulitzer Prize. But she was a noted designer in her own right, particularly in the fields of interiors and garden design. Having spent the first part of her career living and working in the US, she moved to France in 1911 and spent much of her time firstly in Paris, and then at her homes in Saint-Brice-sous-Fôrest and Provence.

Frank Lloyd Wright (1867–1959)

Frank Lloyd Wright studied at the University of Wisconsin, before settling in Chicago in 1887, where he worked for architectural firm Adler & Sullivan, eventually taking charge of its residential portfolio. Wright opened his own practice in Chicago in 1893, designing a series of houses in and around the city over the following years. In 1911 he built Taliesen, a house and studio in Wisconsin; years later, Wright built another studio in Arizona, known as Taliesen West. Among his key projects are the Imperial Hotel (1922) in Tokyo and the Guggenheim Museum (1959) in New York. His many buildings and writings have made

Wright one of the most influential 20th-century architects not just in America, but also around the world.

Russel Wright (1904–1976)

Born in Lebanon, Ohio, Russel Wright initially studied law at Princeton University, while also pursuing an interest in art and design. He worked in the New York office of set and product designer Norman Bel Geddes, before establishing his own design practice in 1927. That same year that he married Mary Einstein, a designer, sculptor and entrepreneur, who became Wright's partner in the evolution of his business and brand, which embraced furniture, home accessories and, most famously, ceramics and dinnerware.

Frank Wynkoop (1902–1978)

Architect Frank Wynkoop was born in Denver, Colorado. By the mid-1930s he had established his own office in Bakersfield, California, northwest of Los Angeles, and later opened an office in San Francisco. Wynkoop became known in particular for his educational projects, designing new schools and extending or remodelling existing buildings. His work includes the Lakeside Union Elementary School (1942) and a series of pre- and postwar buildings for Delano High School. He also designed wartime housing in Bakersfield, San Francisco and Seattle and, in 1943, worked as a designer for the US Navy. Both Wynkoop's son and grandson also became architects.

William Zimmerman (1856–1932)

Born in Wisconsin, William Zimmerman studied at MIT in Massachusetts. He worked with architect John J. Flanders, before opening his own practice in Chicago in 1898, which eventually became known as Zimmerman, Saxe & Zimmerman, after his son Ralph Waldo Zimmerman and son-in-law Albert Moore Saxe joined the firm. For ten years, from 1905 onwards, Zimmerman held the post of Illinois State Architect. He is well known not only for his residential work in and around Chicago, but also for many projects for the University of Illinois and state-funded projects, such as court buildings.

Bibliography

Alba, Roberta de, *Paul Rudolph: The Late Work* (New York: Princeton Architectural Press, 2003).

Andrews, Peter, et al, *The House Book* (London: Phaidon, 2001).

Arieff, Allison, and Bryan Burkhart, *Prefab* (Layton, Utah: Gibbs Smith, 2002).

Arntzenius, Linda G., *The Gamble House* (Los Angeles: USC School of Architecture, 2000).

Boissière, Olivier, *Twentieth-Century Houses* (Paris: Terrail, 1998).

Booth, Hannah, 'Beyond the Forest', *Elle Decoration UK*, March 2010.

Bosley, Edward R., *Gamble House: Greene & Greene* (London: Phaidon, 1992).

-----, *Greene & Greene* (London: Phaidon, 2000).

Boyd, Michael, *Making LA Modern: Craig Ellwood* (New York: Rizzoli, 2018).

Breslow, Kay, *Charles Gwathmey and Robert Siegel: Residential Works, 1966-77* (Boston: Architectural Book Publishing Company, 1977).

Bruegmann, Robert, ed., *Art Deco Chicago: Designing Modern America* (New Haven, Connecticut: Yale University Press, 2018).

Byars, Mel, *The Design Encyclopedia* (London: Laurence King, 2004).

Cambell-Lange, Barbara-Ann, *John Lautner* (Cologne: Taschen, 2005).

Carley, Rachel, *Litchfield: The Making of a New England Town* (Litchfield Historical Society, 2011).

Carta, Diana, *Lake of the Mind: A Conversation with Steven Holl* (Siracusa, Italy: LetteraVentidue, 2018).

Cobbers, Arnt, *Marcel Breuer* (Cologne; Taschen, 2007).

Collins, Brad, and Juliette Robbins, eds, *Antoine Predock: Architect* (New York: Rizzoli, 1994).

Coquelle, Aline, *Palm Springs Style* (New York: Assouline, 2005).

Craig, Theresa, *Edith Wharton, A House Full of Rooms: Architecture, Interiors and Gardens* (New York: Monacelli Press, 1996.

Cygelman, Adèle, *Palm Springs Modern* (New York: Rizzoli, 1999).

Davey, Peter, *Arts and Crafts Architecture* (London: Phaidon, 1995).

Davidson, Cynthia, ed., *Tracing Eisenman* (London: Thames & Hudson, 2006).

Davies, Colin, *Key Houses of the Twentieth Century* (London: Laurence King, 2006).

De Long, David G., 'Bruce Goff's Ford House: Living in Joyful Order', in *Friends of Kebyar* 30.3:82 (2015).

Domin, Christopher, and Joseph King, *Paul Rudolph: The Florida Houses* (New York: Princeton Architectural Press, 2002).

Doordan, Dennis P., *Twentieth-Century Architecture* (London: Laurence King, 2001).

Dow, Alden B., *Reflections* (Midland, Michigan; Northwood Institute, 1970).

Driller, Joachim, *Breuer Houses* (London: Phaidon, 2000).

Dunn, Dorothy *The Glass House* (New York: Assouline, 2008).

Eidelberg, Martin, ed., *Design 1935-1965: What Modern Was* (New York: Abrams, 1991).

Eishenhauer, Paul D., *Wharton Esherick Studio and Collection* (Atglen, Pennsylvania; Schiffer Publishing, 2010).

Escher, Frank, ed., *John Lautner: Architect* (London: Artemis, 1994).

Falino, Jeannine, ed., *Crafting Modernism: Midcentury American Art and Design* (New York: Abrams, 2012).

Fiell, Charlotte and Peter, *Design of the Twentieth Century* (Cologne: Taschen, 1999).

Fox, Stephen, et al, *The Architecture of Philip Johnson* (Boston: Bulfinch, 2002).

Frampton, Kenneth, *Steven Holl: Architect* (Forence: Electa, 2002).

Frampton, Kenneth, and David Larkin, eds, *The Twentieth-Century American House* (London: Thames & Hudson, 1995).

Frank, Suzanne, *Peter Eisenman's House VI* (New York: Whitney Library of Design, 1994).

Futagawa, Yukio, ed., *GA Houses Special - Masterpieces*, 2 vols (Tokyo: A.D.A. Edita, 2001).

Garofalo, Francesco, *Steven Holl* (London: Thames & Hudson, 2003).

Glancey, Jonathan, *Twentieth-Century Architecture* (London: Carlton, 1998).

Goldberger, Paul, and Jospeh Giovannini, *Richard Meier: Houses and Apartments* (New York: Rizzoli, 2007).

Golub, Jennifer, *Albert Frey: Houses 1 and 2* (New York: Princeton Architectural Press, 1999).

Gordon, Alastair, *Beach Houses: Andrew Geller* (New York: Princeton Architectural Press, 2003).

-----, *Weekend Utopia: Modern Living in the Hamptons* (New York: Princeton Architectural Press, 2001).

Gössel, Peter, and Gabriele Leuthäuser, *Architecture in the 20th Century* (Cologne: Taschen, 2005).

Gropius, Walter, *Scope of Total Architecture* (New York: Harper, 1955).

Hansen, Marika, et al, *Eliel Saarinen: Projects 1896-1923* (Helsinki: Otava Publishing, 1990).

Henderson, Arn, *Bruce Goff: Architecture of Discipline in Freedom* (Norman, Oklahoma: University of Oklahoma Press, 2017.

Hess, Alan, *The Architecture of John Lautner* (London: Thames & Hudson, 1999).

Hess, Alan, and Alan Weintraub, *Oscar Niemeyer Houses* (New York: Rizzoli, 2006).

Hines, Thomas S., *Architecture of the Sun: Los Angeles Modernism, 1900-1970* (New York: Rizzoli, 2010).

-----, *Richard Neutra and the Search for Modern Architecture* (New York: Rizzoli, 2005).

Hochstim, Jan, *Florida Modern* (New York: Rizzoli, 2004).

Jackson, Lesley, *Contemporary: Architecture and Interiors of the 1950s* (London: Phaidon, 1994).

-----, *The Sixties: Decade of Design Revolution* (London: Phaidon, 1998).

Jackson, Neil, *Craig Ellwood* (London: Laurence King, 2002).

Jacobs, Kate, 'Take Me Higher', in *Elle Decoration UK*, June 2004.

Jodidio, Philip, *Contemporary American Architects*, 4 vols (Cologne: Taschen, 1993-98).

-----, *100 Contemporary Architects* (Cologne: Taschen, 2008).

Johansen, Ati Gropius 'Designed for Living', in *Historic New England Magazine* (Fall 2003).

Johnson, Philip, and Hilary Lewis, *The Architecture of Philip Johnson* (Boston: Bulfinch, 2002).

Joy, Rick, *Rick Joy: Desert Works* (New York: Princeton Architectural Press, 2002).

-----, *Studio Joy Works* (New York: Princeton Architectural Press, 2018).

Khan, Hasan-Uddin, *International Style: Modernist Architecture from 1925 to 1965* (Cologne: Taschen, 1998).

Koenig, Gloria, *Albert Frey* (Cologne: Taschen, 2008).

-----, *Charles and Ray Eames* (Cologne: Taschen, 2005).

Kundig, Tom, *Houses 2* (New York: Princeton Architectural Press, 2011).

-----, *Works* (New York: Princeton Architectural Press, 2015).

Lamprecht, Barbara, *Richard Neutra* (Cologne: Taschen, 2006).

Levine, Neil, *The Architecture of Frank Lloyd Wright* (Princeton, New Jersey: Princeton University Press, 1996.

Lupfer, Gilbert, and Paul Sigel, *Walter Gropius* (Cologne: Taschen, 2006).

Lutz, Brian, *Knoll: A Modernist Universe* (New York: Rizzoli, 2010).

Lyle, Janice, *Sunnylands: America's Mid-Century Masterpiece* (Chelsea: Vendome Press, 2016).

Lyndon, Donlyn, and Jim Alinder, *The Sea Ranch* (New York: Princeton Architectural Press, 2004).

Maddex, Diane, *Alden B. Dow: Midwestern Modern* (New York: W. W. Norton & Co., 2007).

March, Lionel, and Judith Sheine, eds, *R.M. Schindler: Composition and Construction* (London: Academy Editions, 1993).

McCarter, Robert, *Breuer* (London: Phaidon, 2016).

-----, *Frank Lloyd Wright: Fallingwater* (London: Phaidon, 1994).

-----, *Louis Kahn* (London: Phaidon, 2005).

McCarter, Robert, ed., *On and By Frank Lloyd Wright: A Primer of Architectural Principles* (London: Phaidon, 2005).

McCoy, Esther, *Craig Ellwood: Architecture* (Venice: Alfieri, 1968).

Mead, Christopher Curtis, *Houses by Bart Prince* (Albuquerque: University of New Mexico Press, 1991).

Meehan, Patrick J., ed., *The Master Architect: Conversations with Frank Lloyd Wright* (Hoboken, New Jersey: Wiley-Interscience, 1984).

Meier, Richard, *Richard Meier: Architect* (Oxford: Oxford University Press, 1976)

Melhuish, Claire, *Modern House 2* (London: Phaidon, 2000).

Merkel, Jayne, *Eero Saarinen* (London: Phaidon, 2005).

Mertins, Detlef, *Mies* (London: Phaidon, 2011).

Monk, Tony, *The Art and Architecture of Paul Rudolph* (London: Wiley-Academy, 1999).

Mutlow, John V., *Ricardo Legorreta Architects* (New York: Rizzoli, 1997).

Nakashima, Mira, *Nature, Form and Spirit: The Life and Legacy of George Nakashima* (New York: Abrams, 2003).

Neuhart, Marilyn and John, *Eames House* (Hoboken, New Jersey: Ernst & Sohn, 1994).

Niemeyer, Oscar, *The Curves of Time: The Memoirs of Oscar Niemeyer* (London: Phaidon, 2000).

Noever, Peter, *Schindler by MAK* (Munich: Prestel, 2005).

Pearson, Clifford A., ed., *Modern American Houses* (New York: Abrams, 1996).

Peltason, Ruth, and Grace Ong-Yan, eds, *Architect: The Pritzker Prize Laureates in Their Own Words* (London: Thames & Hudson, 2010).

Pfeiffer, Bruce Brooks, *Frank Lloyd Wright* (Cologne: Taschen, 2000).

Postiglione, Gennaro, ed., *One Hundred Houses for One Hundred Architects* (Cologne: Taschen, 2004).

Predock, Antoine, *Turtle Creek House* (New York: Monacelli Press, 1998).

Robinson, Sidney K., *The Architecture of Alden B. Dow* (Detroit: Michigan Society of Architects, 1983).

Rosa, Joseph, *Albert Frey: Architect* (New York: Rizzoli, 1990).

-----, *Louis Kahn* (Cologne: Taschen, 2006).

Rudolph, Paul, *The Architecture of Paul Rudolph* (London: Thames & Hudson, 1970).

Rybczynski, Witold, *Home: A Short History of an Idea* (London: Penguin, 1987).

Schwartz, Frederic, ed., *Mother's House* (New York: Rizzoli, 1992).

Serraino, Pierluigi, *Eero Saarinen* (Cologne; Taschen, 2006).

Sheine, Judith, *R.M. Schindler* (London: Phaidon, 2001).Shulman, Julius, *Modernism Rediscovered* (Cologne Taschen, 2016).

Smith, Bruce, *Greene & Greene: Master Builders of the American Arts and Crafts Movement* (London: Thames & Hudson, 1998).

Smith, Elizabeth A.T., *Case Study Houses* (Cologne: Taschen, 2006).

Smith, Kathryn, *Schindler House* (New York: Abrams, 2001).

Steele, James, *Charles and Ray Eames: Eames House* (London: Phaidon, 1994).

-----, *R.M. Schindler* (Cologne: Taschen, 1999).

Street-Porter, Tim, *Palm Springs: A Modernist Paradise* (New York: Rizzoli, 2018).

-----, *The Los Angeles House* (London: Thames & Hudson, 1995).

Street-Porter, Tim, and Diane Dorrans Saeks, *Hollywood Houses* (London: Thames & Hudson, 2004).

Sudjic, Deyan, *Home: The Twentieth Century House* (London: Laurence King, 1999).

Thiel-Siling, Sabine, ed., *Icons of Architecture: The Twentieth Century* (New York: Prestel, 2005).

Tinniswood, Adrian, *The Art Deco House* (London: Mitchell Beazley, 2002).

Twitchell, Ralph, and Paul Rudolph, 'Cocoon House', in *Architectural Forum* (January 1951).

Urbach, Henry, *Simon Ungers* (Barcelona: Editorial Gustav Gili, 1998).

Vacchini, Livio, et al, *Craig Ellwood: Fifteen Houses* (Barcelona: Editorial Gustav Gili, 1999).

Vandenberg, Maritz, *The Farnsworth House* (London: Phaidon, 2003).

Venturi, Robert and Denise Scott Brown, *Learning from Las Vegas* (Cambridge, Massachusetts: MIT Press, 1977).

Watlin, David, *A History of Western Architecture* (London: Laurence King, 1986).

Webb, Michael, *Architects House Themselves* (Lafayette, Louisiana: Preservation Press, 1994).

-----, *Modernist Paradise* (New York: Rizzoli, 2007).

Welsh, John, *Modern House* (London: Phaidon, 1995).

Weston, Richard, *The House in the Twentieth Century* (London: Laurence King, 2002).

Weston, Richard, *Key Buildings of the Twentieth Century* (London: Laurence King, 2004).

Wharton, Edith, and Ogden Codman, Jr, *The Decoration of Houses* (1897; New York: Rizzoli/Mount Press, 2007).

Whitney, David, and Jeffrey Kipnis, eds, *Philip Johnson: The Glass House* (New York: Pantheon Books, 1993).

Wilkinson, Hutton, *More is More: Tony Duquette* (New York: Abrams, 2009).

Williamson, Leslie, *Handcrafted Modern* (New York: Rizzoli, 2010).

Wright, Russel, et al, *Russel Wright: Good Design is for Everyone* (New York: Manitoga/Russel Wright Design Center, 2001).

Zimmerman, Claire, *Mies van der Rohe* (Cologne: Taschen, 2006).

Directory

Peter Eisenman
Eisenman Architects
41 West 25th Street
New York, New York 10010
eisenmanarchitects.com

Thomas Gluck / Gluck+
423 West 127th Street, 6th floor
New York, New York 10027
gluckplus.com

Charles Gwathmey
Gwathmey Siegel Kaufman Architects
79 Fifth Avenue, 18th floor,
New York, New York 10003
gluckplus.com

Steven Holl
Steven Holl Architects
450 West 31st Street, 11th floor
New York, New York 10001
stevenholl.com

Rick Joy
Studio Rick Joy
400 South Rubio Avenue
Tucson, Arizona 85701
studiorickjoy.com
Steven Holl
Steven Holl Architects
450 West 31st Street, 11th floor
New York, New York 10001
stevenholl.com

Kendrick Bangs Kellogg
Kendrick Bangs Kellogg Architect
29115 Valley Center Road
Valley Center, California 92082
kendrickbangskellogg.com
Tom Kundig / Olson Kundig
159 South Jackson Street, Suite 600
Seattle, Washington 98104
olsonkundig.com

John Lautner
The John Lautner Foundation
P.O. Box 29517
Los Angeles, California 90029
johnlautner.org

Richard Meier
Richard Meier & Partners
475 10th Avenue
New York, New York 10018
richardmeier.com

Barton Myers
Barton Myers Associates
949 Toro Canyon Road
Santa Barbara, California 93108
bartonmyers.com

Antoine Predock
Antoine Predock Architect
300 12th Street NW
Albuquerque, New Mexico 87102
predock.com

Bart Prince
Bart Prince Architect
3501 Monte Vista NE
Albuquerque, New Mexico 87106
bartprince.com

Simon Ungers
Sophia Ungers
Belvederestraße 60
D-50933 Cologne, Germany
simonungers.de

Gazetteer

This listing contains address and contact details for houses that are open or accessible to visitors. Access conditions to the properties vary considerably, so make sure to contact the institution in question to make arrangements before visiting. Any houses that are featured in this book, but not mentioned here are strictly private and are not open to the public.

Alden B. Dow Home and Studio
315 Post Street
Midland, Michigan 48640
abdow.org

Dragon Rock – Russel Wright
Manitoga
584 Route 9D
Garrison, New York 10524
visitmanitoga.org

Dawnridge – Tony Duquette
1354 Dawnridge Drive
Beverly Hills, California 90210
tonyduquette.com

Eames House – Charles & Ray Eames
203 Chautauqua Boulevard
Pacific Palisades, California 90272
eamesfoundation.org

Wharton Esherick House & Studio
1520 Horseshoe Trail
Malvern, Pennsylvania 19355
whartonesherickmuseum.org

Ex of In House – Steven Holl
137 Round Lake Road
Rhinebeck, New York 12572
tspacerhinebeck.org/visit

Fallingwater – Frank Lloyd Wright
1491 Mill Run Road
Mill Run, Pennsylvania 15464
fallingwater.org

Farnsworth House –
Ludwig Mies van der Rohe
14520 River Road, Gate 1
Plano, Illinois 60545
farnsworthhouse.org

Frelinghuysen Morris House & Studio –
George Sanderson & John Butler Swann
92 Hawthorne Street
Lenox, Massachusetts 01240
frelinghuysen.org

Frey House II – Albert Frey
686 Palisades Drive
Palm Springs, California 92262
psmuseum.org/visit/frey-house

Gamble House – Greene & Greene
4 Westmoreland Place
Pasadena, California 91103
gamblehouse.org

Glass House – Philip Johnson
806 Ponus Ridge Road
New Canaan, Connecticut 06840
theglasshouse.org

Gropius House – Walter Gropius
68 Baker Bridge Road
Lincoln, Massachusetts 01773
historicnewengland.org/property/gropius-house

Healy Guest House –
Ralph Twitchell & Paul Rudolph
3575 Bayou Louise Lane
Sarasota, Florida 34242
Tours are organized through the
Sarasota Architectural Foundation
saf-srq.org

Miller House – Eero Saarinen
506 5th Street
Columbus, Indiana 47201
discovernewfields.org/do-and-see/places-to-go/miller-house-and-garden

The Mount – Edith Wharton
2 Plunkett Street
Lenox, Massachusetts 01240
edithwharton.org

Nakashima Farmstead & Conoid Studio –
George Nakashima
1847 Aquetong Road
New Hope, Pennsylvania 18938
nakashimawoodworkers.com

Schindler House – Rudolph Schindler
835 North Kings Road
West Hollywood, California 90069
makcenter.org

Saarinen House – Eliel Saarinen
Cranbrook Art Museum
39221 Woodward Avenue
Bloomfield Hills, Michigan 48304
cranbrookartmuseum.org/tours/saarinen-house

Sunnylands – A. Quincy Jones
37977 Bob Hope Drive
Rancho Mirage, California 92270
sunnylands.org/visit

Umbrella House – Paul Rudolph
1300 Westway Drive,
Sarasota, Florida 34236
Tours are organized through the
Sarasota Architectural Foundation
saf-srq.org

Index

Acknowledgments

The authors would like to express their sincere gratitude to all of the homeowners, house guardians, architects and designers who have assisted in the production of this book. We would also like to express our particular thanks to the following: Michael Boyd, Carrie Kania, Karen McCartney, John McIlwee, Danielle Miller, Mira Nakashima, Michael Webb, Eric Wynkoop, the staff and volunteers at Sarasota Modern, along with Lucas Dietrich, Fleur Jones, Elain McAlpine and the rest of the team at Thames & Hudson, and Anna Perotti.

To Danielle, Maximilian, Mia and Bosco for your love and support

On the cover: *Front* Glass House (1949), by Philip Johnson
(photo: Richard Powers); *Back* Butterfly House (1951), by
Frank Wynkoop (photo: Richard Powers)

First published in the United Kingdom in 2020 by
Thames & Hudson Ltd, 181A High Holborn, London WC1V 7QX

First published in the United States of America in 2020 by
Thames & Hudson Inc., 500 Fifth Avenue, New York, New York 10110

The Iconic American House © 2020 Thames & Hudson Ltd, London
Text © 2020 Dominic Bradbury
Photographs © 2020 Richard Powers

Designed by Anna Perotti, bytheskydesign.com

All Rights Reserved. No part of this publication may be reproduced or transmitted in any form or by any means, electronic or mechanical, including photocopy, recording or any other information storage and retrieval system, without prior permission in writing from the publisher.

British Library Cataloguing-in-Publication Data
A catalogue record for this book is available from the British Library

Library of Congress Control Number 2020932032

ISBN 978-0-500-02295-5

Printed and bound in Singapore by 1010 Printing International Ltd

Be the first to know about our new releases,
exclusive content and author events by visiting
thamesandhudson.com
thamesandhudsonusa.com
thamesandhudson.com.au